THE
THINKING INVESTOR'S
GUIDE TO THE
STOCK MARKET

Kiril Sokoloff

THE
THINKING INVESTOR'S
GUIDE TO THE
STOCK MARKET

McGraw-Hill Book Company
New York St. Louis San Francisco Auckland Bogotá
Düsseldorf Johannesburg London Madrid Mexico
Montreal New Delhi Panama Paris São Paulo
Singapore Sydney Tokyo Toronto

Library of Congress Cataloging in Publication Data
Sokoloff, Kiril.
The thinking investor's guide to the stock market.
Bibliography: p.
Includes index.
1. Investments. 2. Stock-exchange. I. Title.
    HG4521.S7118   332.6'42   77-29250
         ISBN 0-07-059615-8

1234567890   BPBP   7654321098

The editors for this book were W. Hodson Mogan
and Virginia Fechtmann Blair,
the designer was Elliot Epstein, and the production supervisor
was Teresa F. Leaden. It was set in Electra
by University Graphics, Incorporated.

Printed and bound by The Book Press.

Excerpts from Gustave LeBon, *The Crowd*, reprinted with
permission of Macmillan Publishing Company, Inc.,
New York, N.Y., and Ernest Benn Ltd., Kent, England.

To
A.H.S.
and
B.T.S.

Contents

Contents

Acknowledgments

Many people have helped in the preparation of this manuscript, in one way or another. During the many years that I have spent attempting to fathom the depths of investor psychology, I have received many useful road maps, directions, and lessons.

At the top of the credit ledger are Edson Gould of Anametrics, and his associate Steven Greenberg. Gould's understanding of investor psychology is second to none and is only surpassed by his forecasting results based on that understanding. Richard Russell of La Jolla, California, has one of the most practical (and successful) investment philosophies that I have ever encountered. Just reading Gould's *Findings & Forecasts*, and Russell's *Dow Theory Letters* advisory services has been an education in itself.

Peter de Haas, senior portfolio manager at Lehman Brothers, and William Gordon, an investment consultant in Miami, have been very helpful in imparting to me some of their vast store of knowledge of the market.

Marion Evans and Bill Goldman of Evans/Greengrass, Arnold Schmeidler and Peter Stanley of A. R. Schmeidler & Co.; Bob Ravitz and Dennis Delafield of David J. Greene & Co., and Tweedy, Browne, Inc., all investment counselors, use an exceptionally wise, practical, and successful approach to stock investing.

Acknowledgments

This book has been greatly improved by the addition of numerous charts. For this, I must thank many good friends: Ian McAvity of *Deliberations* in Toronto; Jim Miller of William O'Neil & Co.; Martin Pring of the *Bank Credit Analyst*, David Poole of E. W. Axe & Co.; Ned Davis of J. C. Bradford & Co.; M. C. Horsey & Co.; Gary Shilling of White, Weld; Richard Johannesen, Jr., of Salomon Brothers; *Indicator Digest*; and Bill Jiler of the Commodity Research Bureau.

My heartfelt thanks to all those who read the manuscript and made many valuable suggestions, especially Judith Creedy, Charles L. Grimes, Anthony Gaubis, and David Darst.

I'd also like to show my appreciation to Jim Fraser of Burlington, Vermont, who possesses the largest private collection of investment books in the country, for introducing me to many fine, old books that are now available through his reprint service.

Last, but not least, I'd like to thank all the excellent minds and good friends who have given me time and education over the years, especially Charlie O'Hay; Monte Gordon of the Dreyfus Fund; Bob Salomon, Jim McKeon, and Martin Leibowitz of Salomon Brothers; David Kudish of Hewitt Associates; Ralph Scarpa of Irving Trust; Mike Johnston of Mitchell, Hutchins; Ralph Acampora of Smith Barney, Harris, Upham; Harold Ehrlich of Bernstein-Macaulay; Chet Pado of G. Tsai & Co.; Ray De Voe of Hornblower, Weeks, Noyes & Trask; and Stan Weinstein of the *Professional Tape Reader*.

Kiril Sokoloff

INTRODUCTION

Introduction

After eleven years of widely swinging stock prices, most investors are convinced of the market's madness and randomness. Granted there is a madness to it, as there is to any endeavor where human emotion and crowd behavior are involved. But if one studies and learns about human nature, and observes the behavior of crowds, there is a method in it, too. This book attempts to outline the methods which the most astute stock market professionals have developed over time and through experience.

Those who are successful in the stock market attempt to minimize their risks and challenges. They do this by taking a broad perspective and by *not* trying to predict the unpredictable. Frequently, a forecaster wins many battles, grows overconfident, begins to stick his neck out further and further, finally predicts the Dow Jones Industrial Average will be at such a price at such a time, is invariably wrong, and, as a result, suffers both loss of capital and reputation.

The question to ask yourself is whether you wish to be right about where the stock market is going or whether you wish to make money. The former is a commendable goal, and if you prove correct, it certainly gratifies the ego. But do we participate in the market for ego gratification? Certainly not. We invest in stocks because we hope to earn a good return on our capital, and in the final analysis, our success depends upon how well we invested.

The strategies in this book could have been interpreted in a number of different ways over the past eleven years. Many analysts who use the strategies discussed herein have remained skeptical and cautious about the stock market since 1966, and have kept their assets, for the most part, in short-term money market instruments, with an occasional foray into stocks and long-term bonds. Others, who were willing to take larger risks, have also been cautious, realizing that the 1967–1968, 1970–1972, and 1975–1976 market recoveries were transitory in nature. They rode these market advances for all they were worth, but quickly took profits and avoided a buy and hold strategy like the plague.

The basic reasoning for this cautiousness was that an era had come to an end—for all practical purposes, the postwar stock market advance terminated in 1966. Several farseeing analysts correctly foresaw that the excesses created in that bull market, and the subsequent over-valuation of stocks which occurred in the late 1960s and early 1970s, would have to be corrected. They anticipated this would be a trying period for investors, a time when the deck would be stacked against even the most astute market expert.

But for the first time in eleven years, the odds are improving. The 1966, 1969–1970, 1973–1974, and 1977–197? market declines are starting to create the negative investor psychology that's needed for a real bottom.

However, it is important to remember that no black-and-white formula exists for investing in stocks. Market history shows clearly that as soon as one strategy begins to work well, it invariably takes a fall. If we succeed in leaving you with one thought only, it should be that the *recent* past has little, if any, validity for predicting the future action of stock prices. And, in fact, if the recent past serves any purpose at all, it is to assist us in developing a contrary view—what has just happened, and is well known, is unlikely to occur again for some time. In fact, that is the first lesson of investor psychology.

Other lessons are discussed in detail in this book. We feel that the last chapter of the book is the most important. It is there that we list a large number of questions which investors should ask themselves before undertaking any activity in the stock market. We hope that investors who make serious use of this list will cut their losses significantly and boost their winnings by a large margin.

Kiril Sokoloff

THE
THINKING INVESTOR'S
GUIDE TO THE
STOCK MARKET

Part One
THE FOUNDATION

A GENERAL SUMMARY OF THE STOCK MARKET, ITS
APPLICATIONS, AND MOTIVATIONS

1

The Stock Market:
A Moveable Feast of Knowledge

Knowledge of human nature is a rare gift and a valued quality. If we clearly understand the psychology of humans, then we can go far in predicting how people will react and, thus, get a glimpse into the future. To those who are willing to study and work, the stock market affords an excellent opportunity to observe and learn about human nature. In a sense, it can be all things to all people, depending upon their perspectives.

To begin with, the stock market is simply a marketplace where shares of publicly owned companies are bought and sold. It therefore presents an opportunity for any interested party to invest as large or small a sum as desired in a promising business enterprise.

Let us imagine that you work in the middle management ranks of the telephone company. Let us assume that you have an interest in the ebb and flow of human events and that you think the area of telecommunications is very exciting. You believe it offers unusual growth potential, but you rule out as impractical a direct business involvement. You don't have the capital or knowledge to start a business in that field; furthermore, you're unwilling to risk your security and nice income on the unknown.

But you don't have to risk those things. There's another alter-

3

native available to you—the stock market. You can investigate the relative merits of the few companies involved in that business, study their technology, perhaps even talk personally with company management and the company's customers. If you like what you see and hear, you can buy a piece of the business—by purchasing a few shares of the company's stock.

In a sense, this will give you the best of both worlds. You'll own a portion of a company without having the headache of managing it. Better still, your commitment to ownership can be as large or as small as your judgment, pocketbook, and self-confidence dictate.

But the stock market is much more than this. It can be—to those who know how to read the signs that lie just beneath the shifting sands—a smorgasbord of insights into what is happening in the world. It is a moveable feast of knowledge, a barometer of the temper and times. It is an opportunity to learn what motivates, interests, excites, and controls mankind.

At its most basic level, the stock market is everything that everybody knows about everything. Charles Dow, the founder of the *Wall Street Journal*, believed that the action of the stock market was the sum total of all the knowledge, hopes, dreams, and aspirations of the country.

There are currently some 26 million shareholders in the United States, but interest in stocks is not limited to that number. There are many millions of others who have a vested interest in the stock market, because they are either members of a union or employees of corporations that have pension funds committed to stocks. Thus, the information that is available to the market comes from the farthest corners of the land.

All the information available to the stock market enables it to have a record that is second to none in forecasting the economy. Let's take the behavior of the stock market in the fall of 1974 as an example. At that time, many feared that the Western world, even Western civilization, was heading toward collapse. Stock markets were plummeting; inflation was escalating. There was a lack of leadership all over the world. The United States had a new president (the first nonelected one in its history), and the banking system and business were dangerously overextended.

But by late December of 1974 the stock market was hinting very subtly that the worst would not happen. Then, in January 1975, just as the outlook for business was at its worst, most of the world's stock markets (which incidentally bottomed around the same time in the fall of 1974) took off in a huge upward jump.

To the careful observer, the stock market's action suggested that our economy would soon bottom out. Many others, of course, did not believe what the stock market was saying; they were looking at the rising unemployment, the drop in industrial production, and the bad loans of the banks. But the stock market had seen all those problems and had gone down in anticipation of them. When the market changed direction, it was a signal that we were on the slow road to recovery.

The stock market and the financial markets can be especially useful as a forecasting tool for people in business and can help them in their day-to-day decisions about when to add to inventories, when to cut back on inventories, when to reduce short-term borrowing, when to raise long-term money, when to sell equity, and when to make acquisitions.

So those who "let the financial markets do the talking," so to speak, could have foreseen the inventory recession of 1974-1975. The tip-off was the interaction of the Dow Jones Transportation Average with the Dow Jones Industrial Average. As you can see in Figure 1-1, the Transports peaked out at 278 in early 1972, while the Industrials didn't top out until nearly a year later—at a much higher price (and a new all-time high). So what, you ask?

FIGURE 1-1

(a) Dow Jones Industrial Average
(Courtesy of M. C. Horsey & Co.)

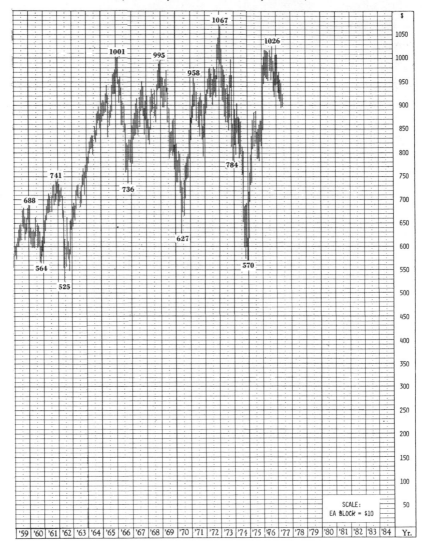

6

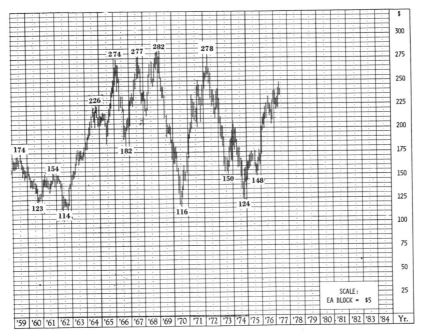

(b) Dow Jones Transportation Average

Well, if you look at the Industrials as representative of the manufacturing capacity of the nation, and the Transports as the selling or shipping capacity, there's an interesting point to be made.

What was happening, according to the averages, was that the fortunes of the manufacturing companies were vastly better than those of the shipping companies. In other words, more goods were being produced than were being shipped. And that's exactly what was happening. But not until two years later did the business community realize it, and only then at a great cost to themselves. Business people had purchased large amounts of raw materials at excessively high prices which, when commodity prices plunged, caused huge inventory losses. Had a businessman been aware that inventories were being overbuilt, he might have cut back on his own inventories and been able to save literally millions of dollars.

7

Some economists and business executives will take sharp issue with the value of the financial markets as a predictive tool. One economist says that the stock market has predicted twelve of the last six recessions. It is natural for economists to react this way to the market, for they look at historical economic data, while the market looks to the future.

In other words, an economist will evaluate third-quarter gross national product figures, or weekly retail sales figures, while the market is looking ahead six months or more. Many economists in 1973, and even through the first six months of 1974, were constantly reiterating how good the economy looked. Such statements as "a soft landing in the valley of the dulls," "the recession we almost had is almost over," and "an oil spasm" are good examples of the thinking at that time. As we all know, there was no soft landing.

The stock market can also be useful to people who are interested in the outlook for cultural tastes. For example, fast-food chains, when compared to the stock market as a whole, have been faring poorly over the last two or three years. This could mean that, in the eyes of investors, the fortunes and the future potential of this industry have been fully discounted or are on the wane. Therefore, one could infer that America's great predilection with the fast-food industry and the fast meal is diminishing.

Bankers can also find the stock market a helpful tool. It can tell them when they should curtail or call in questionable loans, when they should be building up liquidity, and when they should be protecting themselves against a major recession. (On the other hand, it can also tell them when they can safely start making new loans.)

All through 1973 and 1974, bankers made loans to businesses at record levels; some of these later proved to be of questionable worth. Had bankers been serious and successful students of the stock market, they might have seen that a recession was on the way, and they would not have made so many poor loans.

The stock market could also be of some aid to small business-owners. If they understood the significance of market breadth, i.e., the ratio of advancing stocks to declining ones, they could better estimate the future outlook for their businesses. Market breadth, in effect, measures the environment for all business. If more issues are constantly advancing than declining, it's a good sign. (Note that one should take a long view of market breadth, not just day-to-day developments. As a minimum, a perspective of several months or a year should be used.)

That was certainly not the case in the period between the late 1960s and 1974. As you can see from Figure 1-2, market breadth declined throughout—and small business owners had a terrible time. Not only did they have difficulty in obtaining raw materials in 1973 and 1974, but they also were squeezed horribly by the rising cost of those raw materials.

Recent college or business-school graduates could learn something from the stock market. It gives them some indication of the economic outlook for the future and provides them with some idea of which industries appear to have the most potential.

For example, in the 1960s and early 1970s, the consumer sector of the stock market was a stellar performer. New employees who joined a K-Mart or a Sears in 1960 could have had a great opportunity to participate in the future growth of those companies. Had they been able to get options on the company's stock, they would have done really well. But the same may not be true today. Look at Figure 1-3, and ask yourself if the prospects for the industry look as good now as they did back in the early 1960s.

On the other hand, a better future may lie ahead for a company such as American Telephone and Telegraph, which in late 1976 rose to a ten-year high (see Figure 1-4). A young man or

FIGURE 1-2
Dow Jones Industrials and Advance-Decline Line
(Courtesy of Monetary Research Ltd.)

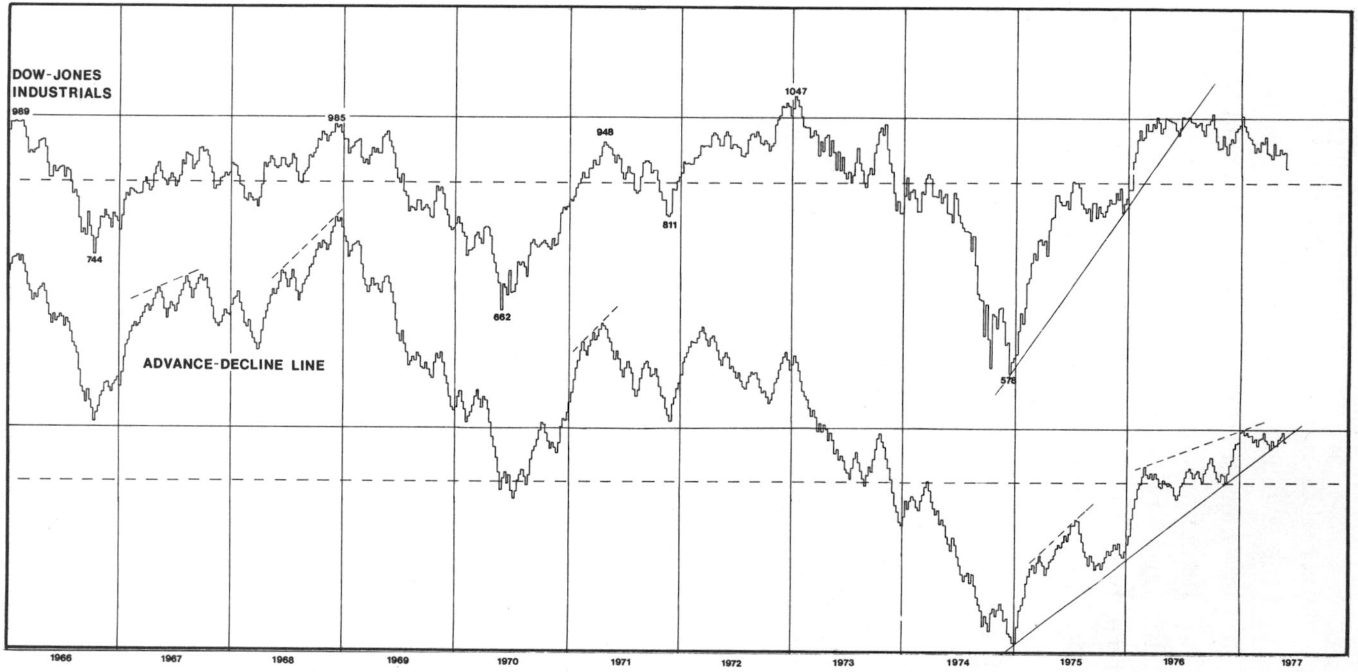

10

FIGURE 1-3
Retail Merchandising
(Courtesy of M. C. Horsey & Co.)

KRESGE (S.S.) COMPANY
MAY DEPARTMENT STORES CO.
PENNEY (J.C.) COMPANY
SEARS, ROEBUCK & COMPANY
STOP & SHOP COMPANIES, INC.
WALGREEN COMPANY
WOOLWORTH (F.W.) COMPANY

SCALE:
EA BLOCK = $15

FIGURE 1-4
American Telephone & Telegraph Co.
(Courtesy of M. C. Horsey & Co.)

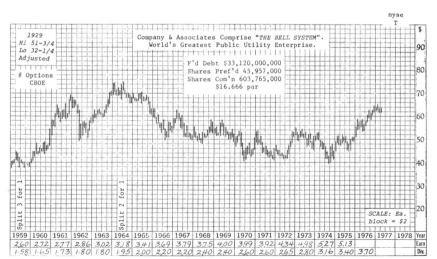

nyse
T

1929
Hi 51-3/4
Lo 32-1/4
Adjusted

Options
CBOE

Company & Associates Comprise "THE BELL SYSTEM".
World's Greatest Public Utility Enterprise.

F'd Debt $33,120,000,000
Shares Pref'd 45,957,000
Shares Com'n 603,765,000
$16.666 par

Split 3 for 1

Split 2 for 1

SCALE: Ea.
block = $2

Year	1959	1960	1961	1962	1963	1964	1965	1966	1967	1968	1969	1970	1971	1972	1973	1974	1975	1976	1977	1978	
Earn	2.60	2.72	2.77	2.86	3.02	3.18	3.41	3.69	3.79	3.75	4.00	3.99	3.92	4.34	4.98	5.27	5.13				
Div.	1.58	1.65	1.73	1.80	1.80	1.95	2.00	2.20	2.20	2.40	2.40	2.60	2.60	2.65	2.80	3.16	3.40	3.70			

11

woman would do well to ask the market from time to time for assistance in job selection.

Even the fashion designer and movie producer can get a helpful hint from the stock market. In 1970, fashion designers came out with what was called the maxidress, a long dress that reached almost to the ankles. As you may recall, it did not do well. The idea behind this dress was that women had become more conservative and were tired of the minidress—but neither the stock market nor any of the other financial markets concurred. Consumer debt was rising dramatically (i.e., the "spend, spend, spend—fly now, pay later" mentality was very strong), and there were no signs of conservatism in the financial arena. Bankers were actually pushing loans, business was madly building inventories, and institutions were in a frenzy to purchase growth stocks.

But now, longer dress styles have come into fashion, and they are quite popular. It is significant that this has happened at the same time that participants in the financial markets are inordinately conservative. "Yield," "total return," and "value" are currently the key words. Speculation of any kind is almost totally absent from the stock market.

If participants in the financial markets are acting conservatively, then can it not be said that the consumer's taste is also becoming more conservative? Thus, the movie producer or mass marketer of books or other products, who is interested in appealing to the common taste, should make a serious study of how this conservative trend will affect the future demand for movies and books and what can be done to give the public more of what it wants.

In summary, then, the market is a great teacher. It offers advice on a thousand subjects to whomever is willing to listen and can interpret correctly. Needless to say, the market can also be very rewarding economically to those who are able to learn its perplexing ways. But, even if you don't make a lot of money in the market, an understanding of how and why it functions can serve you well in other spheres of life. Bernard Baruch claimed that the understanding of human psychology which he learned from his studies of the market was the greatest single lesson of his life and was responsible in large part for his success in government and business.

This study of the market is not easy. The stock market has many faces, masks, false starts, and deceptions. It can confuse you most of the time. Even the wisest and most serious student will be wrong, sometimes egregiously so. Thus, a familiarity with the stock market is not the be-all or end-all. It is merely the beginning.

Yet, study and patience will eventually win out, especially for those who understand what the market is: a study in human psychology. To them, there will be a pattern, a definite logic and order of events.

2

The Motivation of the Stock Market

A long, sustained bull market requires a solid foundation of cheap and ample credit, a deflated debt structure, favorable cost/price relationships and a large pent-up demand for goods and services.

Such bull markets are a natural sequel of a preceding period of declining stock prices and slackening business activity that serve the salutary purpose of eliminating the incompetents, increasing efficiency, eliminating the excesses, and correcting the imbalances built up in the preceding period of rising business activity.

EDSON GOULD, EDITOR OF FINDINGS & FORECASTS AND CHAIRMAN OF THE EDSON GOULD FUND

Discovering the motivating forces of living things is one of man's most profound and challenging tasks. For, to understand the motive, dream, or purpose behind a person or law of life is to gain unusual insight and power.

Napoleon, one of the great motivators of all mankind, understood human nature as few other people have. He learned early in life that the key to the heart and soul of a person is to discover and understand that person's goals in life. Napoleon felt that one could not truly know the character of people by studying their faces or observing how they behave. Character does not show through until well on in life. Thus, it is necessary to probe and learn what people truly want from life. Perhaps they do not even know themselves. Maybe it is only possible to learn the subconscious urge—no matter; in the knowledge of motivation lies control of the person. By appealing to that hidden dream, Napoleon could tie an emotional bond and light a spark to ensure loyalty and dedication.

The same holds true for the stock market. Only after its motivations are understood—completely and thoroughly—can we use its volatility, its Midas touch, and its insight into the future for our own benefit. Since the stock market is fueled and motivated by millions of investors from all over the world, our first step should be to discover what it is that motivates people to buy and sell stocks.

Between 1965 and the present, the stock market, as represented by the Dow Jones Industrial Average (DJIA), has been unable to hold above 1000. This has happened in spite of the fact that earnings and dividends (two things which are normally viewed as determinants of stock prices) are much higher now than they were in 1965. What's more, as you can see from Figure 2-1, earnings and dividends declined in 1958, while stock prices rose. The same thing happened in the 1973–1974 period. It is clear, then, that from time to time other factors have a greater influence on stock prices than either dividends or earnings. These other factors can be reduced to one simple concept: investor perception of value.

In 1968, the last frenzied period in the stock market, investors were willing to pay huge sums for stocks which subsequently were shown to have little, if any, value at all. Conversely, during the 1969–1974 period, when the average stock took a beating, inves-

Figure 2-1
(Adapted from a chart courtesy of *Findings & Forecasts*)

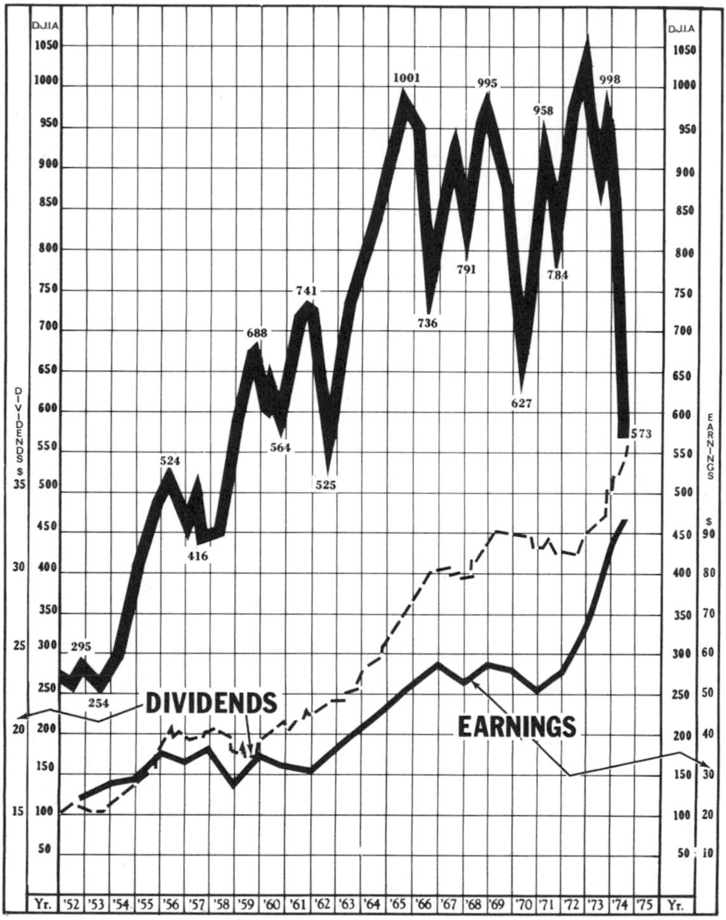

tors' desire to own stocks faded away. (See Figure 2-2 for an unweighted average of some 1500 stocks on the NYSE).

By the time the stock market bottomed in the fall of 1974, most stocks were selling below what some would describe as "known value." Investors ignored the fact that the inflation of the 1970s rendered most companies extremely valuable, if only from the standpoint of replacement cost. The cost of building a new plant,

Figure 2-2
I.D. Composite Index
(Courtesy of Indicator Digest)

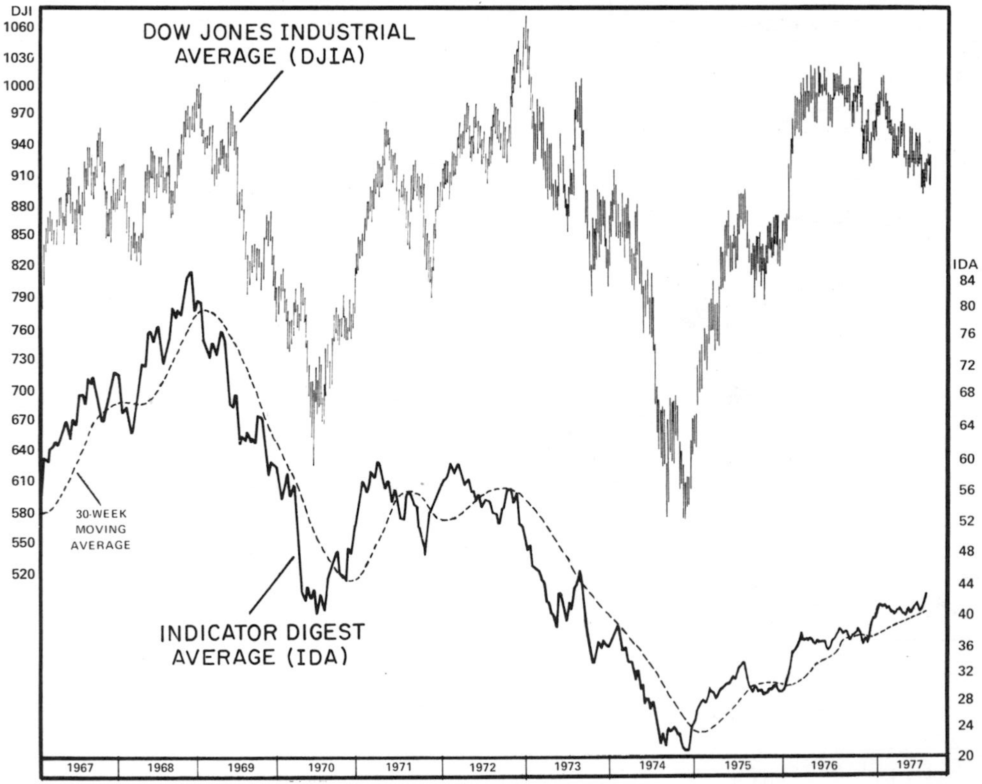

18

opening a coal mine, or putting in a railroad now vastly exceeds the value which the stock market ascribes to companies which own or control such assets. Sooner or later, when the cost of replacing these assets becomes more apparent, investors' perceptions of the value of corporate America could be revised sharply upward. At that time, stocks may once again regain investor favor.

Another way of looking at replacement cost is to deflate stock prices by wholesale prices. Figure 2-3 shows the record going back to 1789. It is interesting to note that the washout at the bottom in 1974 is very similar to that which occurred in 1929–1932, when viewed in this fashion. The drop from 1929–1932 in constant dollars amounted to 69.7 percent. By contrast, the 1974–1975 low amounted to a 51.3 percent decline.

Figure 2-3
Stock Prices in Constant Dollars
(Courtesy of Foundation for the Study of Cycles)

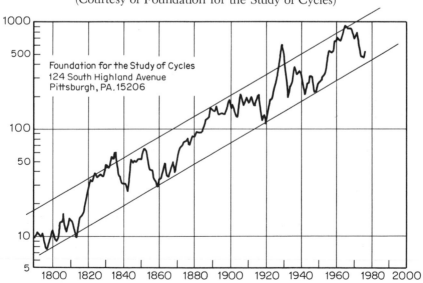

Foundation for the Study of Cycles
124 South Highland Avenue
Pittsburgh, PA. 15206

Investor perception of value can have many facets. Consider a great painter such as Rembrandt, who died penniless and forgotten, or a Johann Sebastian Bach, whose works were eclipsed for almost 100 years by those of his children and grandchildren. Did the paintings of Rembrandt or the compositions of Bach suddenly become more valuable, or did people finally come around to perceiving the lasting value of their works?

Naturally, it must be the latter. Nothing could have altered the basic work of art once it was created. What happened was that the genius of both these men became more widely appreciated over the course of time. Today, an original manuscript of Bach's or a painting by Rembrandt fetches a price that either artist would consider astounding.

In summary, then, the first and foremost motivation of stocks is what investors perceive to be value. During the 1960s, technology companies were much sought after because certain technology stocks had been so successful in the late 1950s and early 1960s. Thus, stories abounded concerning the great profits which could be obtained from technology stocks—and investors were easily persuaded that all technology companies represented value. But, true to form, when a story becomes very widespread, overvaluation occurs, new concepts are launched, weak holders are attracted to the stocks, a shake-out develops soon afterward, and the subsequent decline goes to the other extreme: undervaluation.

Investor perception of value can also be seen in the simple matter of availability of goods. Remember the high price of sugar in 1974? That price occurred because many consumers and business users of sugar panicked at the same time and frantically hoarded unnecessarily large supplies of sugar at inflated prices. (See Figure 2-4.) Before the price of sugar crashed, it reached 66 cents a pound wholesale; recently it was 10 cents a pound. Now,

Figure 2-4

(Courtesy *COMMODITY CHART SERVICE*, a publication of Commodity Research Bureau, Inc., 1 Liberty Plaza, New York, N.Y. 10006)

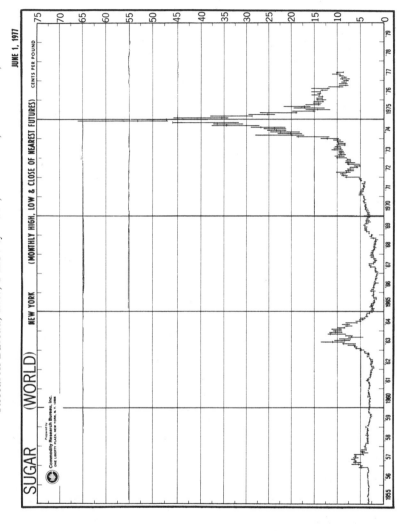

21

who would think that sugar, which traditionally has sold below 10 cents a pound at wholesale, is worth 66, 40 or even 25 cents a pound? Clearly, some did; otherwise the price would never have risen that high.

The same thing happened to copper prices. In early 1973, as you can see from Figure 2-5, the futures price for copper was roughly 60 cents a pound. This price increased substantially in 1973. By the end of the year, copper was selling for $1.00 a pound. In the first quarter of 1974, copper prices reached their peak price of $1.40 and then declined sharply.

Let us return for a moment to the collapse in stocks during 1973–1974. Why did this happen, if dividends and earnings for the Dow Jones Industrial Average were higher than they were in 1966 (when the DJIA first reached 1000)? Here again, it was a question of investors' expectations and perception of value (as well as investment alternatives). Investors weren't looking at intrinsic values; they were looking at the currency disasters and the high rate of inflation. They were listening to the numerous comments being made by the financial media and investment analysts concerning the possibility of another great depression. Because of this talk and these financial threats, investors were moved to sell stocks.

By January 1975, most of the selling pressure was gone. The overwhelmingly bad news had separated all but the most tenacious investors from their stocks. As you recall, the news was terrible: unemployment was rising dramatically, automobile companies couldn't sell cars, and fears of a truly devastating depression on an international scale were widespread. The DJIA knew in advance about the recession and the threat of a financial disaster, and it had fallen from 1051 to 570 in anticipation of it. But now that the selling was over, the market began to look ahead to the economic recovery which began in the first half of 1975. Thus, the market took off in January 1975 and continued upward

Figure 2-5
(Courtesy COMMODITY CHART SERVICE, a publication of Commodity
Research Bureau, Inc., 1 Liberty Plaza, New York, N.Y. 10006)

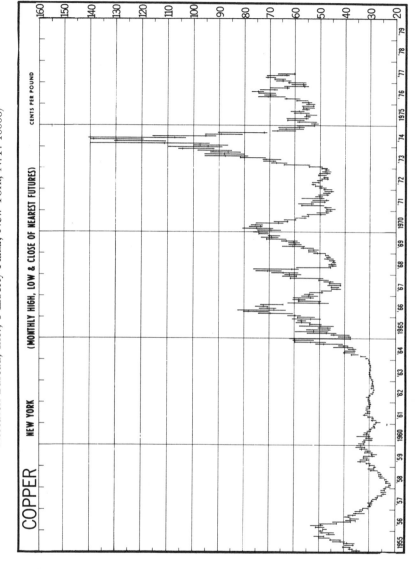

23

almost nonstop until July 1975. During this period, investors were more anxious and eager to buy than to sell stocks, and the supply-demand situation clearly favored an upward trend.

Over time, this perception of value, these expectations of investors, must have a close correlation to reality. Investors can lose their minds in the excitement of panic or euphoria, but sooner or later the truth will out. Just as a nation cannot promote prosperity forever by printing money, so stock prices must reflect over time the economic advancement of the underlying companies.

This advancement is highly dependent on an improving outlook for business, which generally means earnings will rise too. Rising earnings motivate investors to buy because stockholders are part owners of the company in question. Thus, if the business prospers, so, ultimately, will the stockholders. For instance, one of the reasons why the stock market did so well in the first half of 1975 was the unusual turnaround in corporate profits. For the nine-month period ending in December 1975, corporate profits shot upward by some 80 percent, while wage boosts jumped only 6 percent during the period. (See Figure 2-6.)

If a company that starts off with $10 million in annual sales and $1 million in after-tax earnings grows to be a $500 million company with $75 million in after-tax earnings, the original investment in that company will have multiplied many, many times in value. The small amount of capital that was used to buy the stock of that company could well be worth hundreds of thousands of dollars or more.

Of course, some investors prefer that the earnings, or part of the earnings, be paid out to them. This is natural because dividends represent a tangible return on one's capital. Once you have received the dividend, it is yours forever. And if the dividend is raised, the stock price should generally rise along with it, because

Figure 2-6
(Courtesy of E. W. Axe & Co., Axe Castle, Tarrytown, N.Y.)

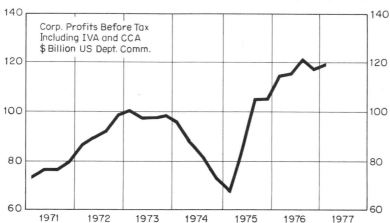

the tangible rate of return has been increased. In theory, the stock price should increase to the point where the rate of return is similar to what it was before the dividend was raised.

This is not necessarily true with earnings: rising earnings do not necessarily mean a rising stock price. Earnings can be manipulated and distorted. Do you remember the conglomerate phase— when the sum of the earnings of all the acquired companies was considered to be greater than the sum of the parts? This was accounting distortion. Add to that replacement cost accounting and the confusion resulting from foreign earnings and inventory profits or losses, and you have problems in determining the true level of earnings. Thus, some investors view the record of dividend payments and increases in dividends as a more tangible measure of a company's financial record.

Besides the financial performance of a company, many other things influence investors' perceptions of value and thus stocks. First and foremost on that list is war. Along with war usually comes currency debasement, because the government doesn't dare to tax and cannot afford to pay for all the war materiel that is needed. Hence, paper money is printed to pay for it. We all know the consequences of a sea of paper money.

If the war is lost, investors stand to lose their entire investment. The company in which they own shares could be taken over by a foreign power; the plant and equipment could be destroyed; the customers of the business could lose purchasing power; or the firm could become a major creditor of a bankrupt government. Even if none of these things happens, capital and interest are diverted away from stocks. Thus, the value of the shares is bound to fall sharply in what would at best be a period of uncertainty.

Another major fear which the stock market has is currency turmoil and inflation. In the 1940s and 1950s, it was said that a little bit of inflation was a good thing. That was probably true—at least as it was envisioned by the people who lived through the great depression and the great deflation of prices that resulted therefrom. But, as a country, we have never been able to do things in moderation. We invariably go to an extreme. So it was natural that, once we started, we would not stop until we got a full dosage.

When costs increase further than companies can raise prices— which happens in the later stages of an inflation—profit margins shrink and financial liquidity is undermined. What's more, large corporations, which are the most visible, are easy scapegoats for the price increases. This adds to the pressure to hold down costs and eats further into profits.

Take utility companies as a case in point. Electricity bills, which are mailed to almost every voter in the nation, are very sensitive politically. It is easy for politicians and regulatory agencies to vote against a rate increase. That action is bound to win more popularity among the voters than a decision which favors the financial soundness of a utility.

Another fear that the stock market has is uncertainty. Just like

Hamlet, the stock market fears "the things we know not of." Upon reflection, this makes a lot of sense. Suppose a good friend of yours comes to you with an idea for an investment and asks you to invest $10,000 in the project. If all of this friend's previous investment suggestions were successful, you would be responsive to the new project, for it could be another attractive venture.

But if an unknown comes to you with a new proposal that you cannot be certain of, and whose record you cannot verify, would you not be very skeptical about investing any money in the scheme?

So it is with the stock market. You would be a very reluctant investor if there were great uncertainties, such as who will win the presidential election, will the Federal Reserve tighten credit, or will Congress move to break up the oil companies. Uncertainty was a major reason why business held back on capital investment in 1976. Government policy on so many levels, from energy to inflation, was so unpredictable as to preclude any certainty. And without certainty, who would want to commit funds to a long-term project? Of course, those who can see through the uncertainty and accurately predict the future stand to benefit greatly from their insight.

The threat of recession, depression, or panic is a very real fear that motivates investors. The memory of these events stays in the unconscious of a nation; even those who did not experience the great depression are aware of it and fear its recurrence. The same is true of a recession, when earnings and dividends may be reduced and the specter is raised of worse things to come. However, for the most part, the worst does not happen, and the pessimists who sell the stocks of solid companies close to the bottom (as the bad news is coming out) live to regret their precipitous action.

Such rational analysis is of little help when the event occurs and it does not keep the stock market from going down or from falling way below a reasonable valuation. Nevertheless, there is a great opportunity for profit during these periods. But investors must be able to see through the haze of fear to ascertain that the selling panic is not justified.

Bernard Baruch said that his faith in the resilience of the economy was one of the main reasons he was able to make a fortune on Wall Street. Growth would resume, he believed, and companies whose fortunes appeared to be at rock bottom would one day thrive again.

The investor who can look beyond the immediate horizon, to the peaks which lie ahead, will be able to capitalize on the worries, the uncertainties, the inflations, the recessions, and the fears of genuine panic, currency turmoil, and war—all of which create exceptional values in the market.

So far, we have talked of stocks in an individual sense. Is there not perhaps a bigger picture, like the evolution of humanity or nations, which affects stocks? The concept of bull and bear markets affords one way of looking at the investment picture on a larger scale.

Let us start off by defining how we see a bull and a bear market. Most investors use the term "bull market" to refer to any rise in stocks, and "bear market" to describe any decline. This is over-simplistic. A true bull market is basically a once-in-a-lifetime occurrence, or at best once in a generation. There was a great bull market between 1921 and 1929, which took the Dow Jones Industrial Average from around 65 to almost 400. Then there was another great bull market which began in 1949 (or 1942, depending on your viewpoint) and lasted until 1966. (See Figure 2-7.)

It is interesting to point to some characteristics of these two periods and to differentiate them from qualities of other "bull moves," which are not the same thing. That is to say, the move off the bottom in 1970, which took the DJIA from 625 to 1051, was not a bull market in the true sense of the word. It was a "bull move," an artificial rise in stock prices which was caused by enormous fiscal and monetary stimulus. That, in turn, was generated by former President Richard Nixon, who, remembering his narrow defeat by John Kennedy in 1960 due to an Eisenhower-induced recession, swore that the same thing would not happen to him again.

One of the first essentials of a long-term bull market is a favorable population trend. This was certainly the case during the 1920s and the late 1940s and 1950s. After both World Wars, the destruction, both in human and economic terms, was so great that massive rebuilding was necessary. One of the first steps that nature took to restore the balance was to promote family formation. As a result, record numbers of babies were born (in relation to the population) after both wars. That, in turn, motivated the purchase of houses, home furnishings, and other consumer goods.

Another thing that is necessary for a long-term bull market is easy credit conditions. Interest rates must be low, so that new projects are feasible economically and interest costs don't become too much of a burden on debtors. What's more, low interest rates are an indication of conservatism, fiscal responsibility, availability of capital, and an absence of speculation and excesses—all of which must exist before a long economic expansion can take place. (Interest rates will also tend to be low if debt burdens are low. Too much debt is a dangerous thing. It means that little additional purchasing power can be created through borrowing. And it poses the threat of a large deflation and debt liquidation, such as we had in the 1930s.)

Another necessity for a bull market to get under way is rampant pessimism, caution, and skepticism. When the reverse—tremendous overoptimism and lack of caution—exists, the stage is set for disaster. The 1920s was one of America's greatest periods of optimism and prosperity. After almost eight years of uninter-

Figure 2-7
Dow Jones Industrial Average

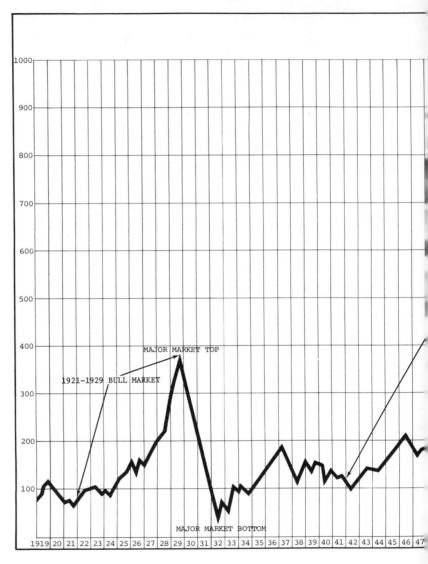

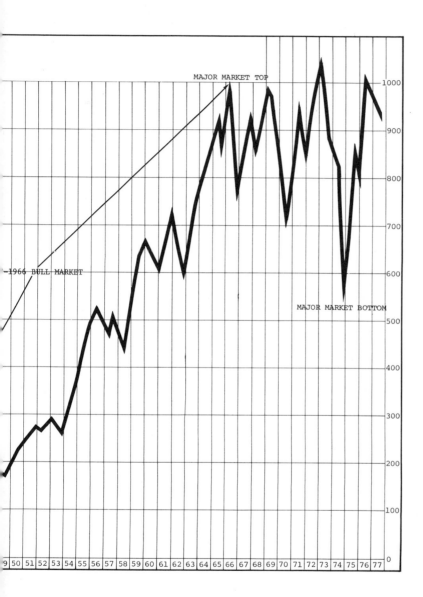

MAJOR MARKET TOP

—1966 BULL MARKET

MAJOR MARKET BOTTOM

| 9 | 50 | 51 | 52 | 53 | 54 | 55 | 56 | 57 | 58 | 59 | 60 | 61 | 62 | 63 | 64 | 65 | 66 | 67 | 68 | 69 | 70 | 71 | 72 | 73 | 74 | 75 | 76 | 77 |

31

rupted economic growth and upward movement in stock prices, no one believed that a recession could occur. No one truly thought that the stock market would stop going up. The expression was frequently used that a new era of prosperity had been entered upon.

The same feeling of euphoria existed in the late 1960s. In 1968, one of the most frequent worries was a "shortage of stock." When one views that concern in the perspective of the 1973–1974 bear market, it seems absurd. Yet people were so overconfident in those days that it made sense to them.

A similar feeling developed among economists in the 1970s. After almost three decades of uninterrupted economic growth, save a few mild recessions, economists and business people had come to think that the government could prevent a serious economic recession. They were convinced that a new era had been entered upon. Hadn't government controlled two recessions (1966–1967 and 1969–1970) right before their eyes? Yet it was this overoptimism, this hubris, both in the late 1920s and in the early 1970s, which resulted in the depression that began in 1929 and the serious recession of 1973–1974.

However, in the aftermath of these serious economic events, business people, consumers, and government become cautious again. Everyone avoids overextension. Banks only make the safest and most secure loans. Business and consumers avoid buying something unless it's really needed. And in this cautiousness is laid the beginning of another period of prosperity.

Another necessity for a sustainable bull market is a long-term demand for goods and services. For example, the great economic expansion of the late nineteenth century was fueled by the railroad boom and the development of the nation's resources. The automobile was an important impetus behind the economic prosperity of the 1920s. Automobiles became accessible to the masses, and almost everyone wanted the freedom and sense of independence that they offered.

The demand for all types of consumer goods, from television sets to dishwashers, helped prolong the great 1949-to-1966 bull market. What's more, business was in consort with government to foster consumption: buy, buy, buy now and pay later. Everything that would make the consumer's life easier was promoted.

All bull markets must come to an end; that is as definite as the inevitability of death and taxes. The questions are, how can we determine what it is that brings them to an end, and what are some of the characteristics that indicate that a bear market might be on the way? (For our purposes, we shall define a bear market as a decline of 30 to 50 percent in the market averages. In other words, a time when selling stocks is warranted.)

First and foremost, of course, are the activities of the Federal Reserve System. The Federal Reserve System was founded primarily to prevent panics and is the mainstay behind our entire credit system. It controls the flow of credit and generally has a large influence on the level of interest rates. According to Edson Gould, editor of *Findings & Forecasts*, since the establishment of the Federal Reserve System in 1913, no bull market has ever ended without a tightening of credit by the Federal Reserve. For example, long before the 1929 crash, the Federal Reserve had started to put the monetary brakes on. But the euphoria was so great and the speculative fires so overwhelming that it took more than a year before the Fed's action had much of an effect.

The same warning signal was given near the end of the great 1949-to-1966 bull market. By 1965–1966, the combination of our military buildup in Vietnam and the launching of new social programs was causing the rate of inflation to accelerate.

The Federal Reserve put the squeeze on in 1966, again in 1969, and again in 1973–1974. Each time, tight credit conditions caused

Figure 2-8
Monetary Policies and Stock Prices
(Courtesy of Anametrics)

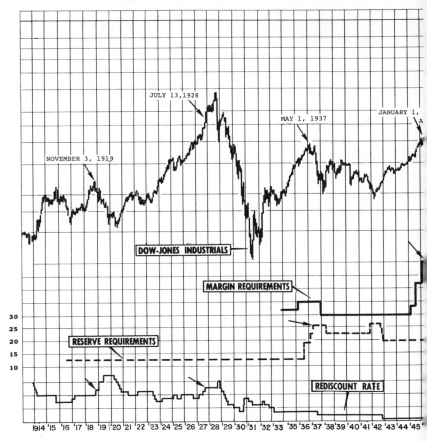

a severe decline in stock prices, although the last decline made the other two look like child's play.

The Federal Reserve can also be a good indicator of a forthcoming "correction" within the confines of a long-term bull market. For example, the Federal Reserve has had some hand in every single market decline since 1919, with the exception of 1937–1938 and 1962. In 1937, one of the reasons was a collapse in commodity prices: the liquidation in the economy had not fully

34

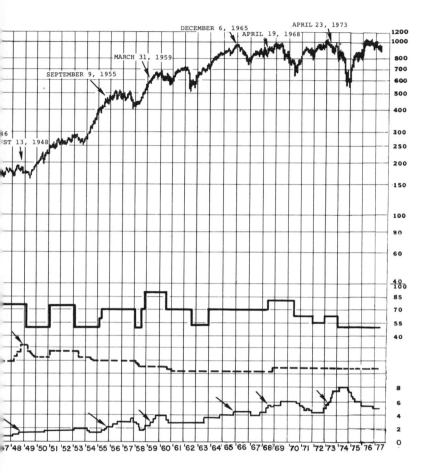

run its course yet. In 1962, the stock market's decline was attributable to Kennedy's confrontation with the steel industry—which, as it turned out, was very prophetic in signaling what later became tremendous antiprofit sentiment on the part of politicians and consumers.

So, in summary, the Federal Reserve and certain monetary indicators, which reflect what's happening on the monetary front, are perhaps the most important areas to watch. Note that the Federal Reserve has three areas under its jurisdiction: stock-market margin requirements (what percentage of a stock's price you can pay for with credit); the discount rate (which is the rate that the Federal Reserve charges its member banks for borrowing at the discount window); and member-bank reserve requirements (the amount of money that banks are required to leave on deposit with the Federal Reserve as a percentage of their total deposits).

Edson Gould has what he calls his "Three Step and Stumble" rule. This rule states that if the Federal Reserve tightens up in any one of these three areas three times in succession, it signifies that the monetary authorities mean business and that a stock-market decline of possibly large proportions could be in the

Figure 2-9
The Record of "The Three Step-and-Stumble" Rule in Action
(Courtesy of Anametrics)

The Rule became activated on ...	By three steps up in the ...	On the previous day the DJIA had closed at ...	The peak registered by the DJIA occurred ...		The subsequent low on the DJIA occurred ...		The DJIA declined to bottoms shown in column (7) ...	
							(8) From peak shown in column (5)	(9) From close shown in column (3)
(1)	(2)	(3)	(4)	(5)	(6)	(7)		
11-3-19	Discount Rate	118.63	11-3-19	119.62	8-24-21	63.90	46.58%	46.14%
7-13-28	Discount Rate	206.71	9-3-29	386.10	7-8-32	40.56	89.49%	80.38%
5-1-37	Reserve Req.	174.27	8-14-37	190.38	4-28-42	92.69	51.31%	46.81%
1-1-46	Margin Req.	192.91	5-29-46	213.36	10-30-46	160.49	24.78%	16.81%
8-13-48	Discount Rate*	179.63	10-26-48	190.88	6-14-49	160.62	15.85%	10.58%
9-9-55	Discount Rate	475.06	4-9-56	524.37	10-22-57	416.15	20.64%	12.40%
3-31-59	Discount Rate	602.65	8-3-59	683.90	6-25-62	524.55	23.30%	12.96%
12-6-65	Discount Rate	946.10	2-9-66	1001.11	10-10-66	735.74	26.51%	22.23%
4-19-68	Discount Rate	909.21	12-2-68	994.65	5-26-70	627.46	36.92%	30.99%
4-23-73	Discount Rate	963.20	1-11-73	1067.20	12-9-74	570.01	46.59%	40.82%
						AVERAGE:	38.20%	32.01%

*Also third increase in member bank reserve requirements occurred 9-24-48.

offing. Gould has researched this back to 1913, and he found its record to be nearly infallible. See Figures 2-8 and 2-9 for the record of the "Three Step and Stumble" rule.

It is interesting to note that tightening by the Federal Reserve often has no effect on psychology or stock prices for quite a period of time. As was the case in 1929, the speculative fires take a long time to be extinguished. Take Figures 2-10 and 2-11 as a case in point. (Any time the Fed tightens one of its three areas of control, there is an arrow pointing downward; any loosening has an arrow pointing upward.) As you can see, in 1945, 1955–1956, 1959, and throughout the 1965–1974 period, the Fed tightened on numerous occasions without any immediate effect on stock prices.

Currency turmoil can also cause stock prices to decline. Currency instability is a great deterrent to the building of confidence that is necessary to promote international trade. The decline in the United States stock market in early 1973 was largely attributable to the then weakness in the United States dollar. In 1975 and 1976 the British pound went into a tailspin, which caused a big break in the London stock market. As a currency declines in relation to another currency, its value declines, and investors became unwilling to put their money into the capital markets of that currency.

Excessive debt can also be a potential troublemaker. This is one of the reasons why the industrialized world has had such a terrible inflation in recent years. Demands of all sorts, domestic and international, were met by the creation of debt. The outstanding debts on the part of consumers, governments, and businesses around the world reached excessive levels while chasing after a smaller amount of goods. That has, in turn, caused inflation.

It is hard to be precise about how much debt is too much, and when one should be cautious. But if the demand for credit—as was the case in 1973–1974—starts to accelerate dramatically, short-term interest rates rise, and bank loans are being extended at high levels, then investors should take heed and be wary. Sooner or later, the excessive burden of debt must be wound down. Debt creation cannot go on forever.

Another cause of bear markets is an antiprofit sentiment on the part of consumers and politicians. There have been many dramatic examples of this around the world in the last ten years. The various regulatory agencies in the United States consistently

Figure 2-10
Federal Reserve Policy
(Courtesy of Ned Davis of J. C. Bradford & Co.)

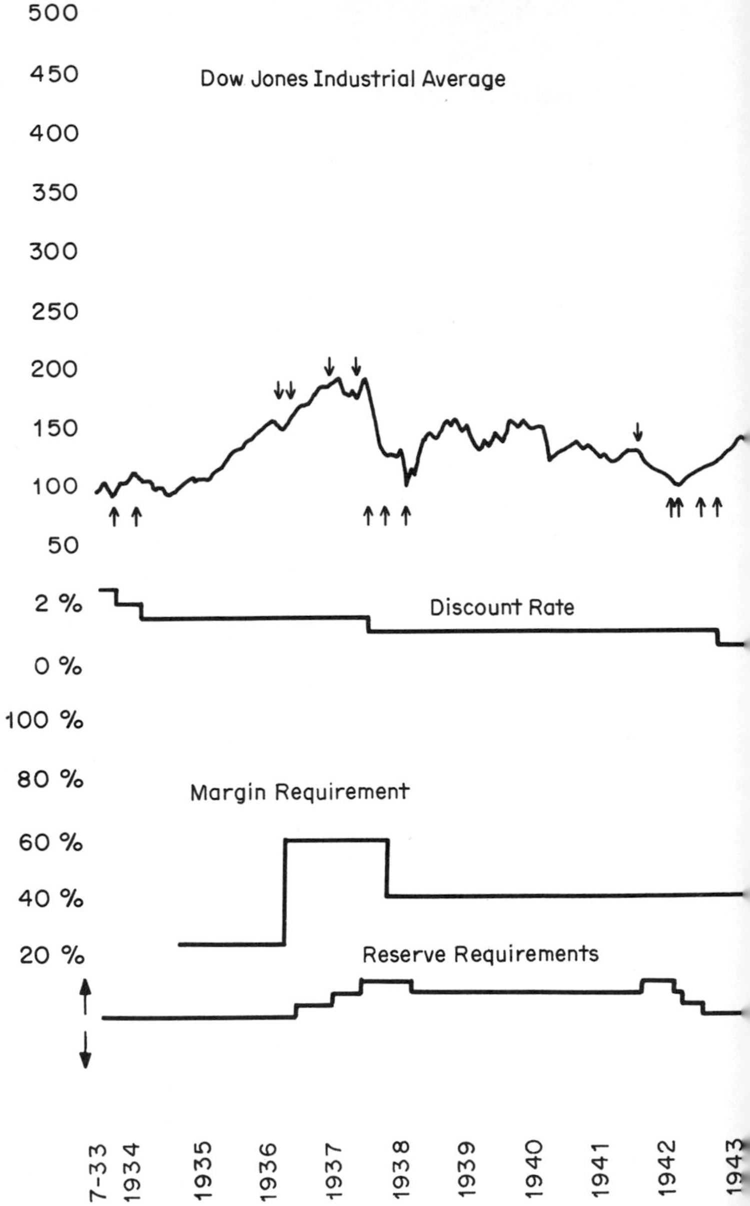

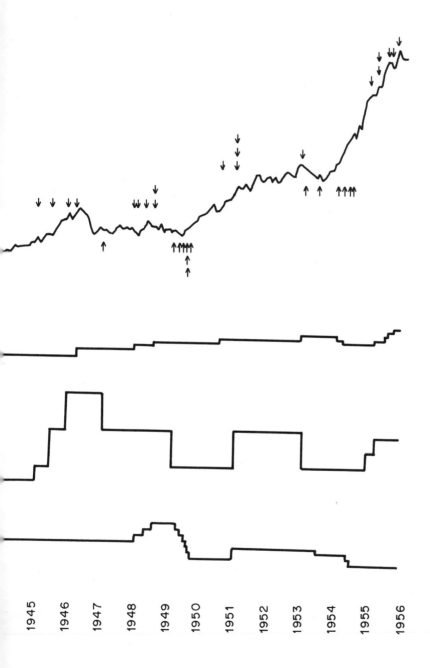

1945 1946 1947 1948 1949 1950 1951 1952 1953 1954 1955 1956

Figure 2-11
Stock Prices
(Courtesy of Ned Davis of J. C. Bradford & Co.)

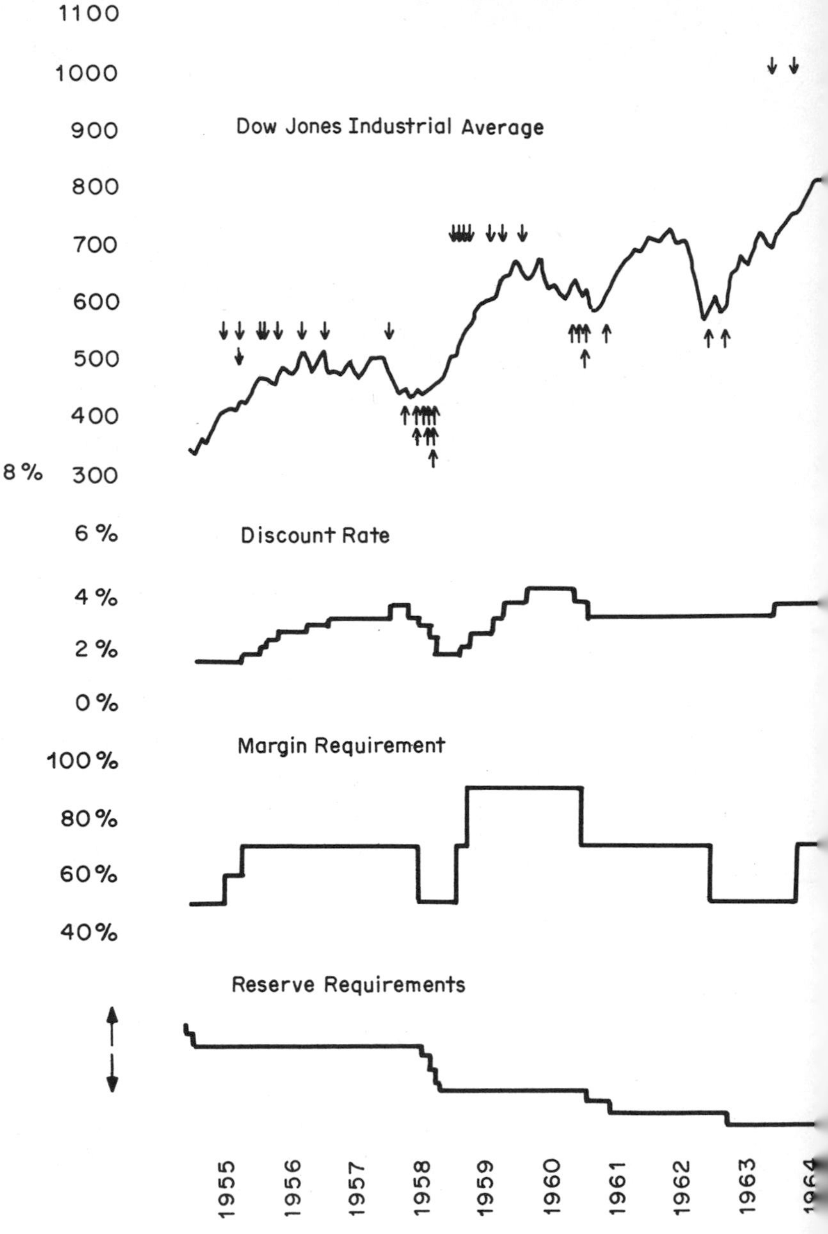

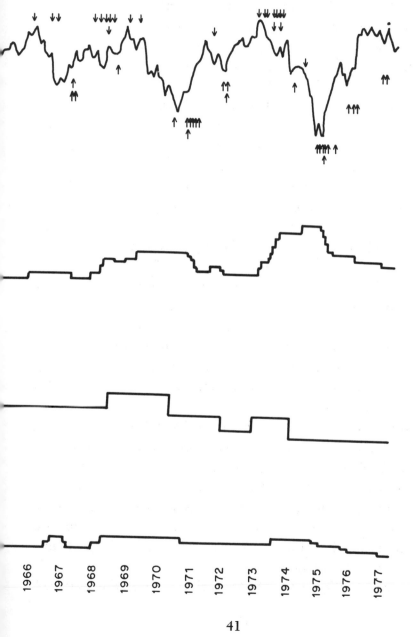

favor the consumer over the shareholder. And as a result, profit margins of publicly held, highly visible companies have suffered, as have dividends as a percent of earnings. This is not a good development, needless to say, for the shareholder.

In retrospect, one would have done well to take heed of the confrontation between Kennedy and the steel industry. It was an accurate forerunner of the antiprofit sentiment that materialized in the late 1960s and early 1970s in this country and elsewhere. (Note that it is a common fault at the beginning of a trend to think things won't get worse. So it was that the French aristocrats believed that the worst was over before the revolution had even begun. The same was true in the 1929 crash. After the first plunge, everyone believed that the panic was over—but it was only the beginning. So, at the first sign of a dangerous trend, don't be too quick to assume everything will soon return to normal. And that is doubly true if everyone else remains unconcerned and breathes a collective sigh of relief.)

Finally, it is important to watch the level of expectations, the level of speculation, and the level of confidence. If things appear to be good, if stocks reflect all the good news that can reasonably be expected to happen, and if everybody is making great sums of money in the stock market, easily and without apparent reason, watch out! This should be an important sign that a bear market may be approaching.

Making money in the stock market is never easy; when it becomes overly so, the game is about to end. This was the case in 1928 and 1929, and again it was the case in 1967 and 1968. In the latter example, Wall Street was bringing companies public at a hundred times earnings. There was widespread stock speculation, and money could almost be picked up off the streets. Yet this "new era" was different from what most imagined: the harbinger of bad times was just around the corner.

The key to getting out of stocks in time is to be able to detach

42

yourself from the mainstream and to evaluate objectively what is going on. This is the greatest challenge that faces investors. It is very difficult not to be swept away by the activities around you, and not to believe what everyone else is drumming into your brain.

But if one remembers that the stock market anticipates good news, and that the smart money always sells the stocks they bought (at much lower prices) under the guise of good news and euphoric business conditions, then one can perhaps avoid many dangers and pitfalls.

The best time, consequently, to buy stocks is when bad news is rampant, pessimism is great, and investors are constantly talking doom and gloom. The time to sell them is when everything appears to be rosy and the preceding problems are long since forgotten and apparently cured.

Life itself swings from one extreme to the other, and so does the stock market, which is nothing more or less than a dramatic example of human psychology. Learn to recognize that there will always be extremes (doesn't the same climate eventually become boring day in day out, year after year?) and try to catch those extremes. Not too precisely, but precisely enough to make a profit. What more could an investor ask for?

Part Two

THE CHALLENGE

WHEREIN THE CHALLENGE TO EACH AND EVERY
INVESTOR IS LAID OUT: CAN YOU PREVENT YOUR
EMOTIONS FROM INFLUENCING YOUR JUDGMENT? CAN
YOU STAY ALOOF FROM THE MESMERIZING, TANTALIZING
INFLUENCE OF THE CROWD? CAN YOU FIND THE TRUTH
ABOUT A STOCK AND ABOUT THE MARKET?

The market discounts, it is interested only in tomorrow. Thus, when a bear market discounts the worst and hits bottom, people are confused because such bottoms invariably occur before they are visible or in any way obvious in the news. News gets to people's emotions, and emotions play a major part in most people's investment decisions. Which is unfortunate, and in a way 'against nature.' 'Why against nature?' you ask. Emotions are totally necessary in your everyday life, emotions will usually steer you right in picking a mate, a friend, in having fun at a party, in deciding what you want to do Sunday, etc. But in the stock market, emotions are the road to disaster. Therefore, your current way of operating as far as learning to live, feel, act, will be a deterrent to you in your investment decisions. You will have to 'unlearn' your emotions when you turn to Wall Street.

Dow Theory Letters
RICHARD RUSSELL

The rank and file of investors must always be led to believe that prices will be still higher—that the real rise is just starting. To make them believe this, the public must have a seemingly good reason. One reason offered in 1929 for probable higher prices was that the best stocks were being picked up by investment trusts, who would hold them for a long period, paying scant attention to intermediate fluctuations. These best stocks would no longer be available at current prices but would soar because of scarcity value. People then became excited and thought: 'If stocks are high-priced because investment trusts are buying them, then why not buy into the investment trusts themselves.' Thus they were led to buy investment trust shares for twice their liquidating value. This meant that they were not merely buying stocks at 30 to 40 times earnings, but at 60 to 80 times earnings!

How Shrewd Speculators Win
FRED C. KELLY AND SULLIVAN BURGESS

3

The Challenge of Emotion

The fault, dear Brutus, is not in our stars, but in ourselves.

Julius Caesar
WILLIAM SHAKESPEARE

As we all know, Benjamin Franklin became one of the great men of all time. But his stature and achievements were the result of hard work and unflinching self-analysis. At an early age, Franklin looked at himself and all his deficiencies and realized that he would amount to nothing unless he improved and changed. He went to others who had more objectivity, and asked them for advice. He sought the truth about himself, no matter how painful that might be. Thus, armed with knowledge of all his deficiencies, he tried to eliminate them. Each week, he'd concentrate exclusively on a particular weakness. The next week, he'd attack another one, and so on. This process of self-improvement went on for years. The result, clearly, was well worth the effort.

How many of us really know ourselves and are willing to subject our true selves to the fierce light of objective scrutiny and analysis? The cocky young business-school graduates who know all the answers have to be put down a hundred times before they

47

see themselves in perspective. The man who believes a woman loves him will go on deceiving himself for years until she finally puts an end to it—and he can no longer delude himself. A beautiful woman, who uses her beauty like a whip, can never find a man to marry her. She cannot understand it, but she won't find a man until she loses her deceptions and gains humility. The young money manager, who's arrogant and impatient and will brook no argument, will lose money until he realizes that he is fallible like everyone else, and must therefore move slowly and keep quiet.

The aspiring writer who thinks she has great talent will keep on writing until someone finally tells her the truth, or until she see it herself. The middle management executive, who thinks he's being passed over by less worthy people, will continue to fall behind until he finds out the truth about himself and changes. The people who lose friends because they are arrogant and inconsiderate will keep on doing so, until they look at themselves honestly and see what they are.

But how to do all this? How to be honest with oneself? How do we get rid of the self-deceptions, the illusions, the dreams, the hopes which cover our true selves and distort reality? That is a lesson that only life can teach.

Some refuse ever to face reality. Others learn very quickly. It is probably something that we are born with, this ability to adapt. But if we don't have it, then we must try to acquire as much of it as possible.

Of all places, the stock market lends itself best to dreams and unreality. There are the illusions of instant wealth with little work. There is the deception that you can make a fortune on Wall Street with little knowledge and study. There is the false thinking that you, and you alone, know what is going on, while the market is lying and deceiving. There is the difficulty of changing your mind (and selling stocks) when you are clearly wrong. As Richard

Russell says, all our weaknesses or faults will come to the fore when we buy and sell stocks—and they will stand between us and success. To win, we must first learn what our deficiencies are, and then find a way to conquer them.

———————————————————

You're sitting in a room with a group of people. One of them launches a vicious dissection of the candidate for office that you support and believe in. At first you remain quiet; then your temperature rises. The remarks are so bitter and unfair that you explode and let loose a blast of emotion.

Your antagonist remains totally unswayed by your remarks and even smiles cynically at your emotional outburst. Later, when you're alone, you begin to think of all the devastating, logical arguments you could have used. Why didn't they come to you in the heat of the moment? Why did you sound off emotionally and not rationally at the time? Precisely because, in the heat of the moment, your emotions took control of your intellect. You were no longer a rational being.

On how many other occasions are we aware of our ineffectiveness under the stress of our emotions? The chess player loses his advantage when he becomes swayed by emotion. The tennis player, the poker player, the boxer, the goalie of a hockey team, the debater, the business executive, the writer, and many others become helpless when emotion takes over.

The author who is overly impressed with the emotion he's trying to express comes between his work and his readers. The tennis player who starts worrying about whether she will win or lose promptly loses because she is "psyched out." The hockey goalie who makes a move too early under the strain of attack stands the chance of having the puck shot by, and into the goal.

The poker player who "loses his cool" and shows his emotions is quickly forced out of the game, owing to his losses. The business person who lets emotions influence an important decision is likely to go wrong. The boxer who loses his confidence and lets fear take over will wind up on the mat.

Psychologists would explain the influence of emotion by comparing it to instinct, which has been bred within us over millions of years of evolution. When threatened, or when something we value highly is put in danger, we react in a certain way—according to how we have been conditioned to react. The instinct for self-preservation is the strongest of all the motivations which work on us, and it is one which only the coolest and most disciplined person can keep under control.

Physiologists would explain that great excitement or undue stress causes the body to work overtime and reduces the effectiveness of the brain. It is interesting to note that many people who accumulated exceptional power (and by inference had great stress) ultimately lost their mental clarity.

Here, from *Napoleon: A Doctor's Biography* by Boris Sokoloff, (Prentice-Hall, 1937), is the physiologist talking:

> It is a coincidence that the "Men of Destiny," who in the history of mankind symbolized supreme power, suffered from the same nervous systems as Napoleon. Julius Caesar and Alexander the Great had the same irritability of temper, the same peculiar paroxysms of fury; both suffered from convulsions and nervous spasmodic movements. . . .
>
> [This] exercise of power, immoderate and excessive as it was, imposed an overwhelming tax on the centers of dynamic energy embodied in (the) endocrine system. The constant and exaggerated demand made upon these glands gradually upset or at least disturbed their physiological equilibrium.

All the more significant becomes the knowledge that these same symptoms were manifested by other dictators as well. This allows us to see in these manifestations a *sui generis* "malady of power" or "malady of Caesars"—a disease which is the consequence of abuse in the exercise of power.

Since politically there are no limits to the power of one man over others, since such domination may become boundless and uncontrolled almost to the point of absurdity, there must be other forces which create obstacles to a single man's supreme domination. Such limitations lie within the man himself—are imposed upon him by Nature. And those who dare to go beyond these physiological limits, who dare to abuse their gift of power, are sternly punished.

Thus we see that humans are innately endowed with an ultimately limited capacity for stress—and highly emotional situations tend to reduce us to impotence. As will become clear, the stock market is an arena where emotion (excitement, euphoria, fear, greed) rules above all else. In the market, we act in concert with hundreds of thousands of other investors, all of whom are susceptible, as we are, to emotion. And because we are a part of this crowd, we lose our identity, we become highly excitable, the adrenalin pulses through our veins, and it becomes hard, if not impossible, to retain rational thought.

You're an independent person. You go your own way and you're fiercely individualistic. You don't like to be told what to do or what to buy. You live in a great nation, a nation of untold prosperity, a prosperity which reaches into the furthest corners of the land. You see this nation begin to spend beyond its means. But things don't stop there. The nation makes promises to everyone, promises it tries to keep on all sides. Economic and social ills can now be eliminated worldwide; all that is necessary is money. So that nation creates money, even where there is none, and distributes it far and wide.

You're a person of common sense, a person who knows history. You're aware that prosperity cannot be manufactured. It cannot be created artificially. You know that the ultimate outcome of excessive money creation is currency depreciation. You resolve to find a store of value. You study more history and you talk to people who have lived through currency debasement. You conclude that gold and gold shares are your only economic salvation. So you put a portion of your wealth into these stores of value.

You are now a person committed—philosophically and emotionally. You watch the debasement continue. Two currency devaluations occur in your great nation, and the stated rate of currency depreciation reaches the double-digit level (the actual one is, of course, much greater).

All around the world, countries are making great promises that cannot, in reality, be kept. Country after country encounters the same problems of inflation and currency loss. But you are happy with your gold and gold shares, for their prices have doubled and tripled from your purchase price. Still, governments don't listen. They won't see the handwriting on the wall. They refuse to alter their ways. So you see no reason to change your investment tactics. You've been right, the government's been wrong.

Suddenly, out of the blue, the gold shares fall in a panic. The selling pressure is so great that certain stocks can't open for trading for several days. You are totally confused, but you figure the antigold interests are responsible for all this. You imagine that the widely publicized sell recommendation of one gold analyst has caused the decline. You fume and rant at the craziness of the market. But you sit tight with your gold investments.

Soon the stock market shoots upward in a burst of glory. All your money is tied up in the gold shares, which slowly drift downward. You are very angry at the stock market now. You claim that it is irrational and dominated by people who don't know what they're doing.

But the stock market continues to rise. And the gold shares continue to fall. You realize this isn't just a flash in the pan. The market rally goes on for almost six months, nonstop. The gold shares have been going down for almost nine months now. But how can this be happening, you ask. We're running the largest peacetime government deficit in history. All the industrialized economies are reflating at the same time. Now we will have inflation for real, you figure. You hold onto your gold shares and watch them march ever downward.

Now, you are really scared. The stock market has jumped upward again in another buying spree. Your gold shares sink day after day. What to do, what to do? It's summer now, and gold bullion plunges: below the halfway point of the entire advance that started at $35 an ounce; below the so-called support levels. Everyone says gold will fall further, from $103 an ounce, where it is now, to $60 or perhaps even lower. What do you do? You panic. You sell your gold shares in one fell swoop. You don't dare look at the confirmation slips. All the profits of past years are wiped out. Half your capital is lost. You are in despair, and you are ready to give up on everything.

What happened? Why did you make the mistake of holding onto gold through thick and thin? For one simple reason. You had become too emotionally attached to alter your way of thinking or your investment strategy. Even though there were reasons to believe that gold was temporarily reaching the end of its good fortune, you refused to look for change, to acknowledge that change might occur.

———————————————————

It's the fall of 1974. The Dow Jones Industrial Average hovers around 600, almost 300 points below its yearly high in January of that year. The young, overconfident money manager is a hero—she's been right all the way down. Many months before, she sold short the high-multiple stocks which came down the most in the recent decline. Several wide-circulation publications have "discovered" this woman, and they are touting her to the skies. She's an important figure, a success story at a young age. She's been smarter than all the banks, the mutual funds, the stock brokers, the insurance companies, the market forecasters, the stock analysts, the economists, and the powers that direct American business. This hero, this woman of great resourcefulness and penetrating insight has tripled her assets and doubled those of her family. She is drunk with success. She dreams of fabulous riches. She visualizes the accoutrements of her financial success: the houses, the cars, the stature.

This woman is so swept off her feet by her self-image and pride in her abilities that she doesn't need to analyze any more. She has an intuitive touch. Her hunches will prove right in the future as they have in the past. So, she takes all the money she's made and all the money she can borrow and she sells short the basic-industry stocks—which she is sure will take the worst beating in the depression that is about to occur.

A month later, the stock market bursts upward, with the basic-industry stocks leading the parade. These stocks charge ahead for six months, nonstop. The woman's gains are now losses. The pride of success is diminishing, but the confidence is still there. She refuses to admit that she was wrong. She holds onto her short position: the market is irrational, and all these sorry bulls will lose in the end. The bearish view will prevail. All that is needed is patience. Isn't she, after all, smarter than all the rest? Didn't she predict the great decline? Wasn't she one of the few heroes? How can she be wrong now?

A year passes. The DJIA now rests at 880, a full 280 points above where she put out the shorts. There are no gains left. All the capital is gone. If she were to cover now, she would lose 180 percent of her capital. She is now humbled, and the wiser for it.

One final point bears mentioning. By pointing out the dangers of emotion, we in no way mean to glorify reason—for reason can be just as misleading as emotion. That's because we are likely to decide we want something and then find a myriad of solid reasons as to why we should do or have the things we wish. As Will Durant says in his book, *The Mansions of Philosophy* (Simon and Schuster, 1929): "Reason, as every school girl now informs us, may be only the technique of rationalizing desire; for the most part, we do not do things because we have reasons for them, but we find reasons for them because we want to do them."

Thus we should always be seeking the truth—the truth about the current state of the market, about the prospects for the companies we own and the ones we contemplate buying. It is only with an intense, objective scrutiny which is very long on analysis and truth and very short on emotion and rationalization that we can make the right decision.

These are some of the challenges (and risks) which the stock market offers. If you are to play this game seriously, and to triumph, you must overcome your emotions, delusions, and rationalizations. We are all fallible. Making money in the stock market is one of the hardest of all the professions. Money will not come easily—and once you make it, you may have an even harder time holding onto it.

4

The Challenge of the Crowd

Who would presume to be above the influence of public opinion? Who has the individual strength to scoff at a common cause? Those who choose to ignore the tides of public opionion are laughed at or ignored. When the economy was at its low in early 1975, were there many left to shout out that massive government deficits were inflationary, ultimately bad for the people, and hence should be avoided? No, we were conditioned to believe that our government could cure economic problems and it was thus entitled to do anything to cure human suffering.

What would have happened to a woman who wore a dress style from the 1950s in the mid-1960s? During the era when long hair was fashionable, there were few men who had the courage (or the inclination) to wear a crew cut.

If you are a young woman who looks attractive in a certain style, do you change without hesitation for a newer style that may be less attractive? If it is fashionable to do so, you might. You may justify yourself by saying that you wanted a change, that you also look attractive in the newer style, and that you're happy about it. Yes, all this is true, but in spite of yourself you have fallen victim to outside influence.

You are a college graduate in 1971. You are anxious to begin work, to start your career and earn money. Yet, many of your classmates go on to business or graduate school. You hear reports that a graduate degree is necessary to get a good job with a high starting salary.

Common sense answers that initiative and hard work breed success, not diplomas. You have a few interviews at corporations, and you hear the same thing: no advanced degree, no job. Soon you give up and go to graduate school. You have fallen under the influence of others. But the arguments in favor of business school were so convincing, you argue. Yes, they always are. That is the power of influence—and, for that reason, its desires cannot be easily denied.

The influence of public opinion—the crowd, mass psychology, social mores, cultural habits, call it what you will—is one of the most profound aspects of our everyday life. Those who would ignore it run a great risk. Trying to predict the future of stock prices or economic events without incorporating the psychology of the crowd is like producing a new product before you determine whether there is a market for it.

Bernard Baruch says in his foreword to Charles Mackay's *Extraordinary Popular Delusions and the Madness of Crowds* (Farrar, Straus and Giroux, 1932) that "all economic movements, by their very nature, are motivated by crowd psychology." Baruch believed that graphs and business statistics were useful in predicting the future outlook for business, but that they left something to be desired. What is not, and cannot be, included in business statistics is the recognition of crowd thinking, of human psychology.

For instance, some analysts are now talking about a new conservative movement in the United States. If, in fact, this trend exists, and persists, it will most certainly affect the consumer's desire for credit and mortgages. And if consumers are less willing to go into debt, then the most recent history of savings rates and consumer debt as a percent of personal income may be misleading.

Thus, a change in psychology, if not plugged into our economic thinking, could vastly alter the validity of our recent statistical experience.

There are those who would promote the thought that stock price movements and (in some cases) economic trends are a function of random behavior, and hence cannot be accurately forecast. It is natural for such a view to become popularized after ten years of widely swinging markets and terrible investment performance. It is the corollary to "You can make a million dollars in the stock market," which was a typical theme of the 1966–1968 frenzied stock-market speculation.

To say that stock price movements or economic events are random (or irrational, which is the implication) is to admit defeat. The stock market was apparently irrational in 1973 and most of 1974, until the economic events occurred which the stock market was anticipating. Likewise, the upward burst in January 1975 was a random movement, totally devoid of logic, until it became clear that the economy was turning around. Where the irrationality comes in is at the end of a movement. The constant repetition of good or bad news always breeds excesses—excesses of fear and of hope. But this characteristic is a rational one, when we acknowledge that human nature inevitably carries things to extremes. It is worth mentioning to those who believe in the randomness of events that the apparent irrational stock movements of 1966–1974 were predicted well in advance by several stock-market forecasters who use crowd psychology as the basis of their investment strategy.

It may be useful to study our most recent madness—inflation—as an example of the potential extremity of events. Back in the 1930s, in the midst of the great depression, the economic problem was diagnosed as an insufficiency of demand. Commodity prices kept falling and falling in a never-ending deflation, dragging down business and farm alike. Anything which could reverse this process was viewed as worthwhile and necessary. Along came John Maynard Keynes, who suggested a handy way to create demand: Let the government spend borrowed money, thereby stimulating the economy. Some give Keynes the entire credit for the popularization of government deficit spending, but the temper of the times is where responsibility should truly be placed. The people and their elected officials were ready for such a scheme. If it had not been Keynes, someone else would have come up with the idea.

Time passes, and this process of deficit spending appears to work. Over the course of the years, economic prosperity resumes. However, this is more a function of the war, and then the pent-up demand for goods and services at the end of the war, than government deficit spending. No matter, the scheme has taken hold of the imagination. Over the course of the next few decades, the idea really is popularized, and it becomes a worldwide phenomenon. Everyone now believes that this is the way to smooth out economic development. We are conditioned to believe it. The crowd is convinced of it, and woe to the person who speaks against it.

As the inflation rate accelerates in the early 1970s, economists talk about ways of learning to live with a high rate of inflation. They might as well talk about learning to live with a cancerous growth in the brain. How can one talk of accepting such a destructive force when it is agreed on all sides that extended and great rates of inflation destroy democracy and democratic institutions? It is an easy matter to end inflation: All government need do is spend only what it takes in. But the deficit-spending idea is so ingrained in everyone's head that it cannot be dislodged. (However, recent events have gone a long way toward returning perspective. It appears that the mass of public opinion is shifting.

Ten years from now we may look back on this era of madness with the same perspective with which our parents viewed the stock speculation of the 1920s.)

In summary, then, the beginning of a movement (i.e., deficit spending in the 1930s) is logical and reasonable. It only becomes illogical, dangerous, and irrational when it is carried to an extreme. And in that extremity, few will stand up against the insanity, for the power of public opinion is too great a force to be reckoned with.

Crowd madness is not a new phenomenon, by any means. It is as old as recorded time, probably much older. Charles Mackay, in *Extraordinary Popular Delusions and the Madness of Crowds*, gives a good account of some of our most extreme and egregious follies:

> In reading the history of nations, we find that, like individuals, they have their whims and their peculiarities; their seasons of excitement and recklessness, when they care not what they do. We find that whole communities suddenly fix their minds upon one object, and go mad in its pursuit; that millions of people become simultaneously impressed with one delusion, and run after it, till their attention is caught by some new folly more captivating than the first. We see one nation suddenly seized, from its highest to its lowest members, with a fierce desire of military glory; another as suddenly becoming crazed upon a religious scruple; and neither of them recovering its senses until it has shed rivers of blood and sowed a harvest of groans and tears, to be repeated by its posterity. At an early age in the annals of Europe its populations lost their wits about the sepulchre of Jesus, and crowded in frenzied multitudes to the Holy Land; another age went mad for fear of the devil, and offered up hundreds of thousands of

victims to the delusion of witchcraft. At another time, the many became crazed on the subject of the philosopher's stone, and committed follies till then unheard of in the pursuit. . . . Money, again, has often been a cause of the delusion of multitudes. Sober nations have all at once become desperate gamblers, and risked almost their existence upon the turn of a piece of paper. . . . Men, it has been well said, think in herds; it will be seen that they go mad in herds, while they only recover their senses slowly, and one by one.

We smile, cynically perhaps, at tales of the Crusades, the South-Sea Bubble, John Law's Mississippi scheme, even the 1920s stock-market madness. That is from another era. Has not the age of science and technology replaced superstition and ignorance? Are we not a thousand times more advanced than our brethren of fifty years ago, let alone two centuries past? We have put a man on the moon. We are close to discovering the secret of life, the magic of prolonging it, of replacing broken-down human organs and of controlling our environment, as no previous civilization has. So, don't talk of crowd madness, you say. We live in a brave new world.

Yes, but for all our accomplishments, we have not changed human nature. It is the same today as it was in 1200 and 1928, the same as during the Crusades and the time of John Law. Nothing has changed except our means of getting to the same end.

Our science and technology make us ever more susceptible to the extreme motions of crowds. Our modern communications system, which transmits one idea or event instantly around the world, is a great contributor to the force of public opinion or crowd psychology.

Alexander Solzhenitsyn, in his Nobel Prize acceptance speech, described our current situation well when he said:

In our most recent decades, humanity has imperceptibly and suddenly become united—hopefully united and dangerously united. So, that a conclusion or an infection in one part is almost instantly transmitted to other parts, which sometimes have no immunity at all against it. . . . What some peoples have already suffered, considered and rejected, suddenly turns up among others as the very latest word.

To deal effectively in the stock market, one must study crowd behavior. One must learn about crowd psychology and always remember that the moment you buy or sell a stock you become part of the crowd. You do not buy a stock in a vacuum, nor can you lock yourself in a dark room after you have made a stock transaction. Good news, bad news, friends, newspaper reports, the direction of the market (and especially your particular stock) all influence your behavior in the market. You can no more divorce yourself from these outside influences than you can remain a hermit or wear a suit of armor.

If, then, we are stuck with crowds, let us try to understand what impresses them, what motivates them. First, crowds don't reason; they don't think. They act on impulse and are highly susceptible to anything new or exciting. As Gustave Le Bon says in his book, *The Crowd* (Macmillan):

It is only by obtaining . . . insight into the psychology of crowds that it can be understood how . . . powerless they are to hold any opinions other than those which are imposed upon them. . . .

Crowds become irrational because they are highly emotional. Sit in a football stadium where the home team is scoring an upset over a hated opponent, and you become overwhelmed by emotion. Go to a rock concert. (Remember Woodstock: Was not the crowd highly emotional?) We have already seen the danger of emotion to reasoned judgment. The crowd magnifies the intensity of that emotion a hundredfold. In so doing, its reason is reduced to that of a blockhead.

No matter how gifted or intelligent we are, the crowd will reduce us to our most elemental instincts and emotions. Twenty-five lawyers together as a crowd will be no more reasonable or farseeing than twenty-five school children. Why is this? Simply because as a member of a crowd, we behave differently than we do as individuals. No matter how dissimilar the members of a group, once they have formed a crowd they become as one.

One way of looking at a crowd is to envision a group or bunch of troublesome teenagers. Individually, one may be reasonably well-behaved and have respect for property. But, as a group, the teenagers tend to egg each other on to see who can perform the most dastardly act. The individual teenagers get courage from each other, and undertake tasks they might never attempt on their own.

Thus, no matter how intelligent a person you are, no matter how carefully thought out your strategy, under the influence of the crowd in the stock market you will most likely be dominated by its emotion. It may be an emotion of fear or of mindless optimism and greed, and it may vary in its intensity.

This last point—the intensity of the emotion—is well worth exploring. For it is this aspect of crowds which determines how great will be the excess (and how irrational the behavior). For the crowd to become overly convinced or excited about a certain thing, there must clearly be preparation.

You don't care who wins a sports event unless you have

followed the fortunes of one of the teams for a long time or if you've bet on the game. How much more exciting it all becomes if your team, a perennial loser, suddenly scores a big win, big enough to send it into the last round of the competition: the world series for baseball, the super bowl for football. How much more exciting still if the opposing team is a hated opponent that has won too much for too long. The pitch of emotion comes if the competition is stretched to the limit and each game is highly suspenseful. That is preparation. The emotions of the partici-pants are built up over a long period of time, until they reach a crescendo of intensity.

The same holds true with the crowd and the stock market. Emotion in a crowd doesn't suddenly appear. It must be carefully prepared. The groundwork must be laid, and the suspense and excitement carefully built up. This happens through repetition of news and example. Thus, if all you hear is good news about stocks, and they go up and up, and others are making fortunes, you too will join in. You cannot stay away. The greater the repetition, the greater the excess, and the harder it will be to remain sane.

In the swing between bull and bear extremes, ask yourself how much repetition there has been. Is the market extremely one-sided, and has emotion taken over? The more extreme the emo-tion, the safer you are in doing the reverse. Thus, if panic is spreading like a fire through a birch forest, you would do well to divorce yourself from the crowd and search for the best value that is being tossed away. Do likewise in a bull market: sell as soon as the repetition of good news has reached the point at which it has created irrationality in the market. Thus it behooves the student of crowds to act only when the crowd has tipped its hand—when the crowd has the bit between its teeth and is taking stocks to ridiculous overvaluation or undervaluation.

How do we measure this? How do we know that the market is

fully in the grip of the crowd and thus acting irrationally? If the market is falling, then we can gauge the influence of the crowd by analyzing precisely how much fear there is around. If one hears vociferous arguments in favor of the worst being past, remain skeptical. The fear has not caught hold yet. If, on the other hand, a bull market is in effect, look for the skeptics and the pessimists. If there is still a healthy group of these, then rest assured that the fever of the crowd has not yet reached a dangerous extreme.

We can also look at the opportunity for repetition. In other words, it's unlikely that the crowd will be swept off its feet without thousands of repetitions. So ask yourself, how much continuity of repetition has there been? If three out of every ten people are unconvinced, more repetition is needed. If nine out of ten agree, then watch out; the crowd is at work. However, this process of repetition may take time. Do not expect an instant reversal. It depends on what has gone before and how quickly good or bad news appears.

Also, watch carefully what appeals to the imagination of the crowd. Lindbergh's flight across the Atlantic was one such event. The RAF's battle against the Luftwaffe was another; so was the racial battle in Selma, Alabama. The world is in a constant flux, and new images come before the public eye all the time. We must note carefully what the public reacts to. If we are able to sense what is next in line (before it becomes too well known), we can bend it to our own use, rather than let ourselves be swept away by it.

To the careful, objective observer, the change in the sentiment of the crowd is usually visible. For instance, there were several sharp drops in the stock market in early 1929 (long before the final crash); the stock-market rally in October 1974 (which took the DJIA up 100 points in two weeks) was an early signal that the bear market was ending; the panic buying that took place in January to June 1975 was an indication of more to come.

66

Also watch where the speculation begins first. What stocks seemed to capture the imagination of the crowd? Whichever area shows an early appeal to mass psychology is the one to concentrate your research on. Try to figure out why it appeals to the crowd. If you think it has true potential for mass appeal, then invest in it—but only between speculative flurries.

━━━━━━━━━━━━━━━━━━━━━━━━━━━━━━━

To summarize, the challenge of the crowd is this: Can we keep our reason when all those around us have lost theirs? No matter how smart or right we have been in the past, we stand to give back all our gains, and more, if we judge the crowd wrong but once.

The pressure may be too much for us, and we should recognize and guard against it in advance. Whatever you do, don't laugh at the power of the crowd. Here is a sobering reminder from Charles Mackay's *Extraordinary Popular Delusions and the Madness of Crowds:*

> Those who had not determined upon the journey joked and laughed at those who were thus disposing of their goods at such ruinous prices, prophesying that the expedition would be miserable and their return worse. But they held this language only for a day; the next day, they were suddenly seized with the same frenzy as the rest. Those who had been loudest in their jeers gave up all their property for a few crowns, and set out with those they had laughed at a few hours before.

Perhaps you still remain unconvinced. You think (and hope) that you'll keep cool when the time comes. There were many who tried to do so in 1929, according to Humphrey Neill in his introduction to Robert Smitley's book, *Popular Financial Delusions* (Fraser, 1963). A group of men from research and economics firms on Wall Street used to meet frequently for lunch at the Old Fire House. During July 1929, this group came to the conclusion that the market was greatly overpriced. And they made a mutual agreement:

> Every man at the table agreed to take advantage of this forecast of experts and to sell every share and every bond that he owned. We each were to make complete liquidation of our holdings no matter whether they were speculative or investment and go "long" on money. Those who were speculatively inclined and who could afford risks could sell "short" U.S. Steel at over 200 and General Electric at 350 and similar opportunities in the "blue chip" field. There had never been such a thorough uniformity of purpose and such enthusiasm for immediate action.
>
> Did we do this and all become rich? No! When the crash finally did come in late October, 1929, and even with some recovery in 1930, I discovered that not one of this group had liquidated his holdings as promised. Some had sold half or less but many who did sell in August or September decided that our forecasts had been wrong and that Fisher, Dice, et al. were right, so they bought back at high prices and . . . well, their academic knowledge was not put to practical use.

So the challenge to investors, above all else, is to remain objective and avoid being swayed by the crowd. Circumstances change as will economic events, but never human nature—and that is what we are dealing with in the stock market. At times, the influence may be overwhelming, but it must be resisted. Under the influence of the crowd, we become mesmerized, and just at the moment when we should be most cautious, we relax. And exactly at the time we should be buying stocks, we are frightened to death and want no part of stocks.

If we are prepared for this pressure, it will help us to some extent. But there is nothing like fear to shake a person's resolve, for this is the most contagious of all emotions.

Being right in the market is often a lonely job: You will have to isolate yourself from your fellows, and that's the hardest thing for naturally gregarious humans to do. We love companionship and like to feel a part of what is going on—isn't this, after all, basic to our biological framework?

5

The Challenge of Analysis
and Perspective

Besides our own weaknesses and our vulnerability to the influence of the crowd, there's the question of what and whom to believe. Every day we're bombarded with thousands of pieces of information, much of which is inaccurate and misleading. One false assumption, one wrong conclusion, can bring stock-market losses.

The honeymoon couple lives in ignorant bliss while the fires of war heat up and threaten to destroy their dream world. The pacifist scientist learns to control the atom, and that knowledge is used to destroy a portion of civilization. The politician passes a law to cure a social ill and, in so doing, creates a greater problem than the one that was to be eliminated. The educator tries to broaden the outlook of the student, but the student only absorbs enough knowledge to become dangerous.

The stock-market speculator buys the right stock at a realistic price, but it happens to be the top of a bear-market rally. The intelligent investor buys the wrong company in the right industry. The seasoned professional is too cautious (at the wrong time) and only trades for a few points a share. The novice buys the wrong company at the wrong time and at the wrong price. The wealthy investor diversifies her portfolio into twenty-five industries, only a

few of which she can monitor closely. The young maverick sells
his stocks at the end of a "correction" because he thinks it has a
lot further to go.

How often in our everyday life do we find that we have made
an incorrect assumption? We believe, like Count Vronsky in
Anna Karenina, that the realization of our dreams will make us
happy—only to find out that it makes us quite miserable. We hear
from a meteorologist that it will rain, so we take an umbrella—
only to discover at the day's end that it did not rain. Or, being
smarter still, we disregard the weather prediction because meteo-
rologists are so frequently wrong, and, as a result, we get sopping
wet. We assume that an associate dislikes us, when he thinks we
dislike him. We live in the country, like Chekhov's sisters, and
believe that going to Moscow will solve every problem.

You are a young woman, bright, ambitious, and, at the age of
30, unusually successful. Every year, you invest some of your
after-tax earnings in the stock market. You've been doing this for
five years, and you have a good record—good enough so that you
sell all your stocks near the top of the market in 1973. You sit on
the sidelines and wait for a good buying opportunity. In August of
1973, with the Dow Jones Industrial Average down more than 15
percent, you decide the time has come. You don't know too
much about bear markets because you haven't personally experienced one. But you think the one which began in early 1973
could be over. You commit all your funds to the market and wait.
Sure enough, the DJIA rallies over 10 percent in little over a
month. Hardly ever does the market look as good. You are
pleased with yourself. Then, the second downleg of the bear
market begins, and the DJIA plunges 220 points in a few weeks.
You lose 20 percent of your capital, but you do manage to get
your funds out of the stock market. What happened? You made
an incorrect assumption: You thought the bear market was over
when it was only beginning, a very easy mistake to make.

Long-term interest rates are still down from their highs, but still are the highest they've been since the Civil War. Does that make bonds a good buy?

Coors Beer has a public offering of stock for the first time ever. It is widely subscribed by Coors devotees. The stock price advances a few points above its offering price, then plummets. What happened? For one thing, the profit margins of all brewers got hit hard. For another, the company was overpriced. Shortly after the offering, the total valuation of Coors was close to $1.4 billion—which is too high when you consider that Anheuser-Busch, the largest brewer in the nation, was valued at $1.6 billion at the time. So, in this case, there were any number of wrong assumptions that could have led you astray.

It is the easiest thing in the world to make a wrong assumption. And it is even easier to be misled by people who don't know what they're talking about, or who understand the issues but reach the wrong conclusion. There are several research analysts on Wall Street who do brilliant detail work, incisive analysis, and invariably come to the wrong conclusion.

Our world is so complex today that we are inundated, and at times overwhelmed, with detail. We discover that what used to be a simple matter of industry outlook now involves knowledge of government regulations, antitrust action, consumerism, patent infringements, foreign competition, product obsolescence, and so on. Who has the expertise to really know the inner workings of one industry, let alone a score of industries? And if the experts following the industry have trouble devising a successful stock-market strategy, what hopes do we have? Furthermore, even if we gain access to someone who is an expert on a subject, will that someone come to the right conclusion? And couldn't that conclusion prove to be wrong, if it weren't interwoven with the economic and stock-market cycle?

In summary, then, we must first eliminate as many assumptions as possible. Only in this way can we reduce our potential for errors. Second, we must know where we are in the economic and stock-market cycle. If we don't, all the other work we do can be negated. We must study the signposts of the cycle to determine where we are. Third, we must learn how and where to get our information. We must discover sources that are reliable and whose quality of information and analysis is above reproach.

Part Three

RISING TO THE CHALLENGE

WHEREIN SOME SUGGESTIONS ARE MADE AS TO HOW WE
CAN CONTROL OUR EMOTIONS, REDUCE THE INFLUENCE
OF THE CROWD UPON US, AND MINIMIZE INCORRECT
ASSUMPTIONS.

If emotion, susceptibility to the crowd, and wrong
assumptions are the biggest dangers in the stock market, can we not devise methods to circumvent them?
Can we not extract our emotions and any unnecessary
assumptions from our activities and our decision-mak-
ing process? Can we not learn how to retain our heads
while others are losing theirs?

What school child has not heard Rothschild's comment
on stocks: only buy them when there is blood in the
streets. Yes, we can all see how that works. But how can
we forget about the "blood in the streets" and concentrate instead on value? And how can we be sure there
won't be more blood in the streets? How can we make
sure that we shall have adequate funds or liquidity to
take advantage of the value created by the blood in the
streets? (Maybe we have retained a full line of stocks all
the way down.)

There are answers to these questions, but they do not
lend themselves to a specific formula. You do not buy

stocks after 29½ straight days of declines, nor should you sell after 2½ years of a bull market. Remember, we are dealing with emotions and crowds, neither of which can be categorized in any simple way.

In the next nine chapters, we shall attempt to give answers to some of these questions, although we make no magic promises.

6

How to Tell Where You Are in the Bull/Bear Market Cycle

Few investors buy at a bear-market bottom, and even fewer buy the right stocks and hold onto them for the entire bull market cycle. The same is true for bear markets. Few, if any, sell at top prices. That is what bull and bear markets are all about. Neither is accommodating, and both strive to go as far along the road as possible without public participation.

Take, as an illustration, the end of the bear market in the fall of 1974. At that time, short-term interest rates were above 10 percent and provided a powerful disincentive to consider stocks. For that reason, many investors rejected stocks and bonds, even though they thought the markets were due for a rally. In short, there was no viable reason to buy stocks; to do so was very uncomfortable and nerve-wracking. As subsequent events bore out, stocks were a much better investment at that time than short-term money-market instruments.

What happens if you missed a major bottom, or if you want to invest money during the middle of the next stock-market cycle? How can you get your bearings and then judge the life expectancy of the bull market?

The first step in answering these questions is to ask yourself how obvious and how large the current economic problems are.

77

If they are enormous, seem unsolvable, and together provide a heavy disincentive to buy stocks, then the odds both of safety and of longevity are probably on the investor's side. In the 1930s, for instance, the country was faced with an overwhelming unemployment problem, deflation, and debt liquidation.

There appeared to be no way to solve the unemployment problem, and no way to cure the terrible devastating deflation. How could commodity prices be raised enough to keep the farmers from bankruptcy? How could confidence be restored in banks and in business? How could purchasing power be increased? And so on. But, as always happens, a cure was developed for these problems—and we currently are reaping the evil crop which was planted in those years. No doubt, at some future time, our cure for inflation will create a devastating deflation.

In general, then, a good time to buy stocks (or to make investments) is when the bad news is overly apparent, and the future appears to be very dim indeed. And, therefore, the less appealing that stocks seem, the greater the risks apparently attached thereto, and the deeper the pain in your stomach when you've bought a stock, the better your decision probably is. Conversely, the easier it is to decide, and the more obvious the attraction of stocks or a particular stock, the more questionable your action becomes. The hardest and most painful decisions will be the best ones.

In making a decision to buy stocks, be sure to consider carefully whether all the bad news is out, and whether stocks have discounted all the potential bad news. For example, as we mentioned earlier, during the 1929–1932 market decline, each market drop was hailed as the end. But the end didn't come quickly; it went on and on for almost three years. In retrospect, this was not so surprising, given what had gone before.

Thus, one way of measuring whether the worst is over is to analyze how great were the excesses which existed in the period before. So, if one were looking at the French Revolution and one were aware of how egregious was the absolutism, the luxury of the nobles and the king, and how great were the suffering and poverty of the commoners, it would be apparent that no quick solution would be possible. No mere constitution or declaration of human rights would suffice.

Take the case of a Napoleon or a Hitler. After disrupting all of Europe and killing millions, would anything short of total surrender be adequate?

In the 1920s, the stock-market frenzy was beyond anything that had happened before or has happened since. The aftermath would not be gentle. Let's try to recapture the spirit of that period and envision for a moment the magnitude of the excess, so we can more fully comprehend the need for a lengthy, painful, and protracted reaction.

First of all, in the summer of 1929, there was a host of men and women who had come to Wall Street and burned their bridges behind them. At some predetermined level of paper profits— $50,000, $100,000, $200,000—these people had given up their jobs and careers to devote themselves full-time to the pursuit of money. Part of these paper profits had already been spent on new homes, jewelry, and other luxuries. The prevalent atmosphere was one of indescribable excitement, magic, and easy living. It was almost as if the stock market were there solely to satisfy the dreams, hopes, and aspirations of thousands of players who believed they were owed a living.

Stock prices kept going up and up in unrealistic fashion. By mid-September 1929, the averages had risen by 35 percent since the beginning of the year; they had jumped 71 percent since the end of 1927 and 123 percent since the end of 1926.

Business, too, was surrealistic. In the month of August 1929, steel production rose 18 percent above the previous record for August; consumption of cotton in August exceeded its August record by 6 percent and loadings of railway freight were the second largest on record for *any* month.

Such increases in expectations, stock prices, and business performance could not last: They were not sustainable. And, needless to say, the return to realistic expectations would take a long time.

Could this kind of unreality be wiped out overnight? Could a mere 50 percent drop in the Dow Jones Industrial Average from 386 to 200 (which occurred in the October-November crash) wipe out these excesses? No. And just as the market became so unrealistically overvalued in 1929, it became equally undervalued at the bottom in 1932—and actually remained that way for many years. But this is all perfectly natural. By its very nature, each action breeds an opposite and equal reaction. We are all victims of Newton's laws.

Another way to ascertain whether the market has discounted the worst that can happen is to evaluate how widespread the pessimism is on the part of consumers, the business community, and politicians. In late 1974, for example, despair straddled the nation like a great colossus. Major publications carried cover stories discussing the possibility of another great depression; there was widespread talk about either runaway inflation or a massive deflation.

If such talk persists for several months, and stock prices do not decline in the face of it, it is possible, indeed probable, that all the bad news has been discounted. It is usually a fact of history that neither the best nor the worst that is expected to happen occurs. It is the unexpected event that no one anticipated that is so dangerous and destructive.

(I might here add a personal note. In early 1974, an analyst I know became increasingly partial toward the view that a major deflation was the great risk facing our economy. He was attracted to the view because everyone talked only about inflation, its dangers, and its inevitable continuation into perpetuity. This feeling was so widespread that he became concerned that the real risks lay in the other direction—that consumer and business spending power would be so sapped by inflation and loss of confidence that buyers would go on a strike.

But in late 1974, he began to view the major deflation theory as less and less likely. Even though economic events were shaping up as he had feared they might, two things persuaded him otherwise. The first was an advertisement for a newsletter which he received at home. The cover of the envelope said, "How to protect yourself from the coming depression." He figured that any event which had received that much recognition just wasn't going to happen.

The second event was a re-reading of Bernard Baruch's book, *Baruch: My Own Story* (Holt, Rinehart and Winston, 1957), wherein Baruch tells of how he got out of the market before the 1929 crash. Although Baruch felt a bear market of sorts might develop, he said that he didn't have the slightest conception at the time of the depth and duration of the coming stock-market and economic contraction. In other words, if Baruch, one of the few men to make a fortune on Wall Street and hold onto it, couldn't foresee a great depression when it was right on top of him, how could we lesser mortals ever perceive it? Many analysts in late 1974 and early 1975 were arguing the case for an even more severe contraction than 1929-1932. It seemed hard to believe that they all had such brilliant insight. Those two simple observations were the keystone for my friend's move from bear to bull.)

There were other simple ways to reach a similar conclusion. For instance, several commentators were able to pick the precise 1974 bottom because they were watching closely how the market reacted to bad news. One analyst, for instance, turned bullish in December 1974 (the absolute bottom) after having been bearish for almost ten years. He based his decision on the following analysis: He noted that companies cut their dividends, yet their stock prices failed to react. In other words, he perceived that the selling was drying up, and that stocks had nowhere to go but up. He also noted that the ratio of advancing issues to declining issues was improving markedly from the negative to the positive for the first time in close to ten years. (This is another simple way of measuring selling pressure.)

It was incidents like these which persuaded this analyst that the worst was over and that the selling pressure was complete. The concept here is that people anticipate that something is going to happen—a runaway inflation, a financial disaster, a panic—and they sell their stocks in advance. When the actual event occurs, there are very few people left to sell stocks, and just a little bit of buying power can drive the market up.

There is something psychological about the unexpected event which makes it worse in the imagination than in reality. Have you ever worried about losing your job? Remember the sleepless nights, the worries, the pain in your stomach? Suddenly, the worst happens: you do lose your job. You begin searching for another one and in a matter of weeks you are feeling better. Once the worst happens, you can't worry about it anymore; you can't blow it up to excessive proportions. It is the same with the stock market: When the worst that can happen actually happens, there is a collective sigh of relief.

Imagine a tug of war between two sides, the bulls and the bears. The bears gradually gain momentum and pull the rope away from the bulls. Eventually, the bulls become disheartened and only a few are left to tug on the rope. The bears are ecstatic now and run off, carrying the poor bulls behind them. When victory is assured, the bears lay the rope down to celebrate. Overconfidence breeds lack of caution. Suddenly, the bulls pick up the rope and march a long ways before the bears can mobilize themselves again. This is what happens at a market bottom.

7

Where Are We in the Current Stock Market Cycle?

Most people have forgotten what a real bull market is like. In fact, anyone who is younger than 30 years of age today has probably not personally experienced the power of the bull. It is therefore hard to imagine that Bethlehem Steel rose from 20 to over 600 during the boom which came about because of the First World War. Equally hard to conceive is that the Dow Jones Industrial Average jumped nearly sixfold during the 1920s, an event roughly equivalent to a surge in the DJIA from 570 in 1974 to 3500 in 1982. Forgotten also is what some consider the greatest bull market of all time, when the DJIA rose more than ten times between the 1942 bottom of 93 and the 1966 top of 1001. It is generally thought that such price action is from another era and won't occur again. It may take many years, but it will happen. (See Figure 7-1.)

In fact, in the years ahead we may enter a great period of American economic history, a time of surprising prosperity. It is hard to believe that such a thing is possible when one looks around at all our problems—the threat of accelerating inflation (or deflation), the worldwide pyramid of debt, the instability of international currencies (with frequent devaluations and disruptions), the energy crisis, the inhibiting tax structure, and the apparent inability and unwillingness on all sides to solve these problems.

FIGURE 7-1
The Stock Market Cycle

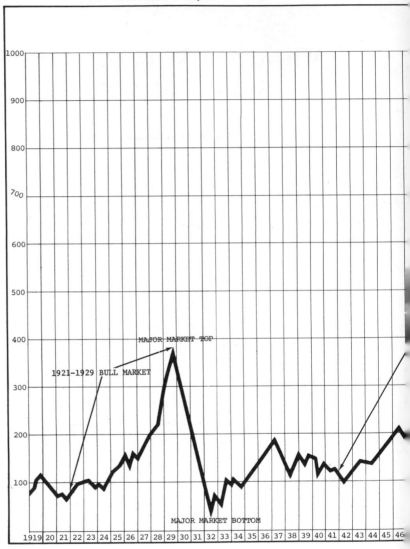

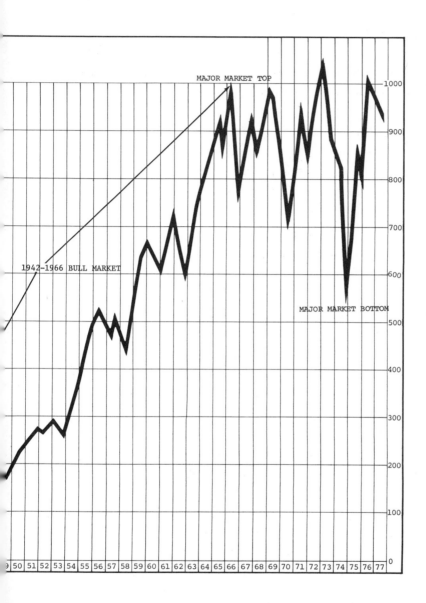

But a familiarity with history shows that such problems are eventually faced and overcome. The first major prerequisite to their solution is an acknowledgment of their existence. And that we most certainly are seeing. Hardly a day goes by without widespread publicity concerning the overwhelming adversity that we face today.

Major publications point to the tens of billions of dollars worth of loans to underdeveloped nations and imply that there is some question as to their repayment. Every small upturn in short-term interest rates is thought to be the first step on the road to interest rates of 10 percent. One bad report on monthly wholesale or consumer prices is heralded as a return to double-digit inflation. Recessions seem to lurk behind every corner. And President Carter has launched a massive public-relations effort to convince us of the gravity of our energy shortage.

It is precisely because such attention is being given our economic troubles that they may be less of a problem than we think. For example, a business person who continuously expects short-term interest rates to head up again will do everything possible to protect against that eventuality: build up a cash position, sell bonds with a long maturity, and avoid, if at all possible, borrowing money from banks. And, in taking such action, each business person will make a small contribution to stable interest rates.

The same holds true for inflationary expectations. If the business community or consumers believe inflation is about to accelerate, they will plan accordingly. Business people will reduce inventories, build liquidity, and pay off short-term debt. Consumers will cut back on spending, pay down debt, and increase savings. Such steps could forestall and, if we are lucky, prevent a recurrence of inflation. Thus, caution and skepticism are healthy signs in our economy and in the stock market.

Because pessimism is so widespread and the stock market has

performed so poorly over the past ten years, few investors are interested in stocks. At the bottom of the bear market in the fall of 1974, the most broad-based market indexes (when deflated by the rise in prices) had fallen some 80 percent from their highs. What's more, the decline in the market has lasted for almost eight years now, which has tended to discourage even the most tenacious investors. What we are left with is the start of a foundation from which a bull market could be launched in the years ahead.

It is worth pointing to some fundamental changes that are taking place in the economy and the world we live in which suggest that better times may lie ahead.

First and foremost is the fact that the great inflation which began in the 1940s may be on the decline, and for all practical purposes may be finally brought under control. For one thing, as you can see from Figure 7-2, all inflations come to an end. This is a firm fact taught by history. Many people today believe that inflation will never end—this is especially true among the young, who have known nothing but inflation. But history tells a different story. Also the behavior of bond prices in 1975–1976 argue strongly against continued inflation. Bonds are a good measure of inflationary expectation because they offer a fixed return and are very sensitive to any change in the rate of inflation. Hence, when the rate of inflation is declining, investors require less of an inflation premium, and the prices of bonds are bid up.

The Dow Jones twenty-bond average, composed of ten industrial bonds and ten utility bonds, gives a hopeful illustration of inflation's demise. This average and its predecessor index, the Dow Jones forty-bond average, had been in a declining trend since 1946, when the Full Employment Act was passed and our great inflation began. But, as you can see from Figure 7-3, the Dow Jones twenty-bond average rose above a previous peak in late 1976 for the first time in many years (actually, since before

FIGURE 7-2
Inflation 1749-1974
(Courtesy of White, Weld & Co.)

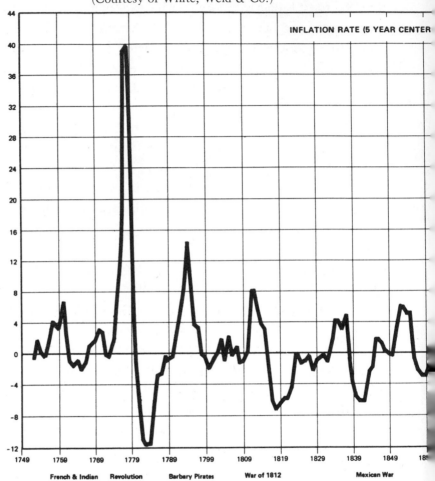

1946). That is a significant event and an indication that a major reversal in trend could be under way.

The implications of a stable price environment are practically inestimable. Consumers, business people, and investors will all benefit. Mortgage rates will decline, and homes will cost less. Real purchasing power will increase, instead of decreasing as it

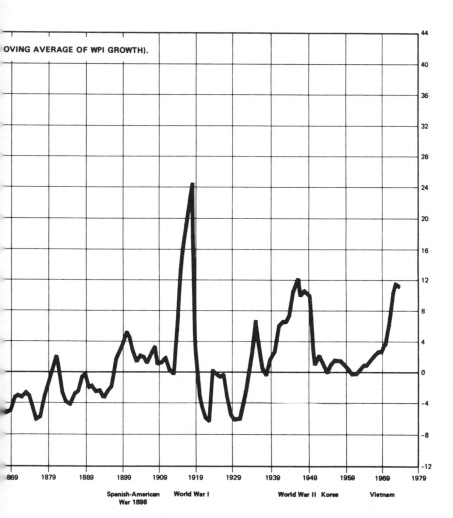

has for the last ten years. As a consequence, consumers will have more money to spend; business will have more profit to reinvest in plants and equipment, and more money to pay out in dividends.

A stable economic and price environment is the best of all possible worlds for investors, because the stock market likes

FIGURE 7-3
Dow Jones Twenty Bond Average
(Courtesy of M. C. Horsey & Co.)

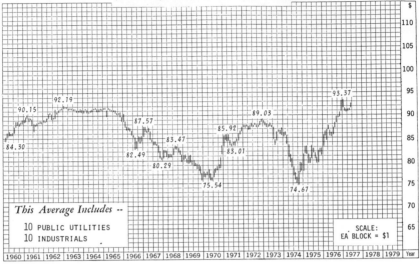

stability and certainty more than anything else. In fact, the last time we had such a stable environment was in the 1920s, and we all know what kind of a bull market took place during that period. (We don't mean to imply, however, that there won't be inflation scares or declines in the bond market in the years ahead.)

Let's use a very simple illustration to make this point. Assume a company has doubled the price of its products because of inflation. A doubling in sales price, coupled with a restoration of the original profit margin, leads to a doubling in after-tax earnings and a doubling in earnings per share. (And that's not even assuming that actual unit volume could increase with a concomitant jump in profit.)

Thus, if the company's stock were to sell at the same relationship to earnings as it did before the inflation began, its price would double. However, price/earnings ratios (the price that an investor is willing to pay for future earnings) also tend to rise during periods of price stability. So, there is the possibility of even further appreciation potential down the road.

The other interesting development, and one of considerable significance, is what may be the beginning of grass-roots support for capital formation. (Simply stated, capital-formation supporters promote the making of capital as a necessary ingredient for the creation of jobs.) This trend, if realized, could be the first major turning point in our financial development since the "welfare state" and Keynesian economic policies came of age. Those policies and those ideas have brought us to the present sorry state of world affairs, where inflation has eaten away at our wealth and given us no real benefit in return: The poor people are still poor, and the poor nations are still poor. It is the obvious failure of these old policies which will have to push us eventually toward more of a free-enterprise approach to economics.

It is not unusual for nations to go through periods of great capital formation and then great capital disintegration. It is necessary and, in one sense, good. The laggards of society, in a relative sense at least, are given an opportunity to catch up to the "great achievers."

If the power of the world and the wealth of the world were held exclusively in the hands of a few, there would be no new markets to sell products to and rapid growth of the world economies could not continue. So, from time to time it is a great boon to long-term economic growth to slow down individualism so that participation can be greatly widened and increased.

We have just been through such a period. Many, many people who had no access to education or opportunity have had a fair chance to advance. Other countries around the world have now seen our economic "miracle" and want the same for their peoples. All this implies that a greater and greater number of people will be able to contribute to the world's economic development in an effective way. Productivity will ultimately jump, as will international wealth.

If, indeed, capital and profit will no longer be dirty words in the years ahead, business people and investors will benefit greatly. The wealth that has been hiding during these many years of confiscatory tax policies will once again be able to surface and be used productively. And wealth will be allowed to accumulate without prohibitive taxation. Part of this wealth will go into the stock market, because ownership will once again be a respected right.

There is not and there will never be a shortage of capital per se. The critical factor is whether there will be capital available at any price if there is a danger of taxation and expropriation. It now appears that the leaders in the West are starting to realize this fact and may eventually press capital formation as a means of creating jobs.

Another way to look at the capital-formation question is to make an analogy to the stock market. A stock-market move is usually punctuated by what is called a "correction" or a "retracement" of the initial advance. A retracement is normal if its extent is no more than one-third to two-thirds of the initial advance. In other words, if a stock goes from 30 to 60, and retraces one-third of the move, i.e., to 50, the upward trend of that stock is still considered to be in force. Perhaps this country has just seen a one-third retracement of its initial upward advance, which began in the nineteenth century and ended in 1932.

During that first move we had tremendous gains in industrial technology, and we rose to first place among nations. Unfortunately, as a result of that advance, too much power and too much wealth were accumulated in the hands of too few—and we needed to spread the wealth and power. That is what has now effectively happened, and we may be preparing for another primary move whose strength and duration no one can yet foresee.

It could last a long time, and the end result could be exceptional prosperity for the United States and those who are willing to invest in its future.

One more favorable aspect of our promising future in this country is the present makeup of our population. The baby boom which began in the aftermath of the Second World War is now coming of age. Although some of these people already hold jobs, the vast majority are still unemployed. They have yet to make homes or buy furniture, household goods, and cars. Some analysts estimate that 15 million people will be looking for jobs between now and 1982. (When you realize that the total number of employed persons in West Germany is only 20 million, you can appreciate what this means in terms of potential demand for goods.) We shall have to have unusual economic growth to find jobs for these young people. And, as they enter the work force and purchase necessities, they will contribute to economic growth.

Over the longer term, of course, one must be prepared for an ultimate market top, and a time will come when stocks should be sold. How long that will be is anyone's guess. But it is possible that stock prices could eventually reach heights that today appear ridiculous.

By that time, America will probably have regained its strong position in the world. The problems of inflation will have been solved; worldwide currency stability will be in effect. The rest of the world, especially those nations that are not industrialized, will be following closely in the United States' footsteps and importing our technology, management, and resources.

But as all that good news begins to overwhelm the public consciousness, investors should start to look for potential problems. When good things start to happen, everybody relaxes and the groundwork is laid for financial disaster and bear markets. When caution is thrown away, bankers lend money to weak corporations and finance impractical business projects; governments decide to spend money unwisely in attempts to solve problems that cannot be solved; and consumers forget their cautiousness about saving and go on frenetic buying sprees.

When these developments occur, investors should be very wary. Even though their timing may be off by a year or two, they should seek liquidity and some type of liquid investment. Investors who got out of the stock market in early 1928 may have suffered some very unpleasant times during the next year and a half, but their judgment was redeemed in later years. (And, no matter what happens, remember how insidious the market can be, always setting a trap for those who have been smart. Many who escaped in 1928 were lured back in 1929 just in time for the crash, and many who got out in 1929 were sucked back in by the 1930 rally—which is where the real fortunes were lost.)

Hence, it is very important not to be too greedy and not to expect too much. The investors who sell too early are always the wise ones. Hanging on for top dollar is the shortest way to ruin. Don't quibble over a few points; take your profits while you can.

8

The Search for Value

You work hard all year. You slave and slave, all in the name of taking a long vacation to Europe. All your savings, all the hard work, goes to one thing only. The time comes at last and you spend six weeks of bliss in a foreign land. When the trip is over and you're back, you ask yourself, "Did I get value, was it worth it?" If you have no regrets, then it was. If the value of that trip more than equaled every second of hard work, the sacrifice was worth it—to you. If you'd do the whole thing over again, you got value. Others might not agree with your view of value, but that's not the point.

The stock market is always fluctuating up or down as people's perception of value changes. One day everybody wants basic-industry stocks; the next day nobody wants them. One moment everybody chases growth stocks, then no one does. The way around these fads and this whimsicality is to look for stocks that have intrinsic value.

The question for any potential investor is, "What will have the most lasting value of all the investment alternatives you see around you?" What is truly necessary? What do people really want, and what will they continue to want? What new process or machine can make us more productive (which seems to be the general direction and evolution of the Industrial Revolution)? What product or service will satisfy long-term and growing needs?

Certain styles of dress will catch on for a short period and then die away as quickly as they came. A type of drink comes quickly into favor, rapidly replacing another line that recently was the latest thing. In a general sense, drinks and clothes serve a basic purpose: alcohol is the opium of the people, and fashionable clothes the expression of vanity. Thus, neither of these will become obsolete. But the superficial manifestation of the desire for drink or clothes will change all the time. In other words, one can invest in a fad or one can invest in something of lasting value. Would you rather acquire an interest in a machine that makes platform shoes or a company that sells all types of shoes? The more lasting the value, the more likely it is that your investment will work out.

An early investment in the automobile industry brought fortunes to those who had the clairvoyance to see the future. Likewise, anything tied to autos, such as tires, glass, and oil, also made fortunes for many. Those who saw the potential at an early stage, who recognized the possibilities and held through thick and thin, did much better over time than the quick shooter who bought and sold and always looked to maximize short-term performance by participating in the latest fad. For those who are past masters at human psychology, the short-term method might get good results, but it takes exceptional talent, ability, and a lot of luck. And the odds are against you.

It's much easier to take a long-term view. What is the future outlook for society? What do people want? What are they likely to want? What will satisfy their needs? And then, what company, what industry, will supply those needs?

When you look at things from that point of view, the investment choices are cut down a lot. In the 1949–1966 period, you were operating in a consumer society, where consumption was promoted and everyone wanted to have all the latest goods and appliances. It was a relatively sure thing that companies supplying those needs would do well. But now we are in a different environment. Consumers are now up to their ears in debt. And the growth in consumer spending will probably not be able to continue at past rates. We must look in a different direction now.

There are many types of values on Wall Street, and one should keep them all in mind when contemplating an investment. There is, first, the value of the current return. The current return or dividend is paid to you quarterly and can never be taken away. Once you get it, you put it in the bank or spend it.

But what is an adequate rate of return? In the late 1940s, investors were disillusioned with stocks. No one thought the market would ever come back, and stocks were in some cases yielding twice as much as bonds. This value sat there unrecognized, unnoticed for many years. Yet that is one of the key criteria of value: It cannot be immediately perceived. If it were, then it would no longer be such a value. Everyone would be after it, and the value would be gone overnight.

Next is the value of growth. As we'll see in a later chapter, the compounding effect of return on capital can generate literally astronomical rates of capital appreciation. The trick is to find an investment that will grow. You don't want a company that will just grow tomorrow; you want a company that will grow for ten years or more. And who knows what the world will be like ten years from now? Hence the difficulty in picking a true growth company.

Then there's the value of assets. You can buy a company which owns or controls assets which you think are undervalued. They can be assets in the ground, such as coal, uranium, or copper. Or they can be corporate assets, the assets on the balance sheet minus the liabilities.

In line with all this, it should come as no surprise that the three best measures of value in the stock market are book value, dividend yield, and price/earnings ratio. Let us briefly look at each one of these.

Price/earnings ratios, which measure what investors are willing to pay for a dollar's worth of earnings, are a good measure of expectations and, hence, value. If price/earnings ratios are low, so are expectations, and vice versa. Needless to say, stocks should be bought when price/earnings ratios are low, and sold when they are high.

As you can see from Figure 8-1, price/earnings ratios below 10

FIGURE 8-1
(Courtesy of Schabacker Investment Management)

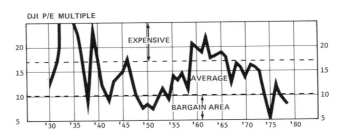

are an unusual occurrence. In fact, price/earnings ratios for the DJIA have only fallen below 10 on three occasions in modern stock-market history. (Note that the 1932 bottom was a unique situation—the earnings of the Dow Jones Industrial Average were in a deficit, and hence price/earnings ratios at that time rose to infinity.) The three occasions were 1942, 1949, and 1974. These three dates are significant in themselves: 1942 was the beginning of the war-induced bull market; 1949 was the start of the great postwar bull market, and the rally from the 1974 bottom was one of the sharpest advances of all time.

Price/earnings multiples do not lend themselves to black-and-white analysis, as some other measures of value do. But it is important to remember that a recent study of price/earnings ratios between 1871 and 1971 showed the average monthly price/ earnings ratio of the market to be around 14. Thus, any extreme deviation from that, in one direction or the other, should be a signal for caution or for buying. A good rule of thumb is this: A market that is selling below 10 times earnings is worthy of serious consideration, and a market that is selling at 17 to 19 times earnings calls for caution. Of course, these parameters may not apply to individual stocks with unusual growth potential.

Now let us look at book value, or shareholders' equity per

FIGURE 8-2

(Courtesy of Schabacker Investment Management)

share. As you can see from Figure 8-2, whenever the DJIA sells close to its book value, it represents an unusual value. Only three times in over forty-five years has the DJIA sold below book: in 1932, at the bottom of the Great Depression; in 1942, when western Europe was being overrun by the Nazis; and at the bear-market bottom in 1974. Clearly then, stocks offer good value when they are selling close to book value.

Next is the value of $1 worth of dividends. (See Figure 8-3.) Some analysts find this to be the most useful gauge of value. The

FIGURE 8-3

(Courtesy of Schabacker Investment Management)

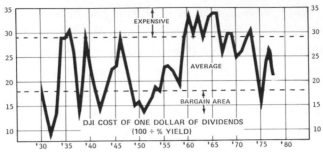

thinking here is that dividends represent the most tangible form of return on investment, and hence are the best measure of investor expectations. Thus, when expectations are low, investors will require a higher dividend yield; and when expectations are high, a low one. A good way of measuring dividend yield is to establish a "price/dividend ratio," which, in effect, measures what investors will pay for $1 worth of dividends. Simply put, a 10 percent yield implies that investors will pay $10 to receive $1 worth of dividends. A 5 percent yield suggests a value of $20 for $1 worth of dividends. If the price/dividend ratio of the DJIA falls below 18, the market is considered undervalued. This has only happened on five occasions since 1930: in 1932, 1938, 1942, 1949–1951, and 1974. These years all correspond to major bear-market bottoms. A good rule of thumb is that a price-to-dividend ratio below 18, or roughly a 5½ percent yield for the Dow Jones Industrial Average represents good value. Conversely, a price/dividend ratio around 30 (which represents a 3 percent yield) is representative of an overvalued market.

It is worth noting that the average yield for the stock market between 1871 and 1971 was 4.83 percent. Clearly then, any extreme variation from that figure should put investors on notice.

Of course, in any study of dividends, one must consider the

payout ratio of earnings. Higher payout ratios imply the possibility of higher dividends which suggest higher stock prices. The average payout ratio for blue chip companies over the last 100 years has been around 67 percent. Thus, when dividend payout ratios are significantly lower than 67 percent, there is a chance that the payout ratio will increase in the years ahead.

You might well ask, what happens if book value, price/earnings ratio, and dividend yield conflict? Which of these should carry the most weight?

The answer would have to be dividend yield. Over time, price/earnings ratios and book value may not be as useful as dividend yields. For instance, at the end of the postwar bull market in 1966, price/earnings ratios were fluctuating between 13 and 17, not an unusually dangerous level. (As you can see from Figure 8-4, the highest price/earnings ratio for the DJIA, 24, occurred in 1962.) But the yield on the Dow Jones Industrial Average fell to around 3 percent at the 1966 top—a good signal of overvaluation.

Moreover, during the 1969–1970 and 1966 lows, dividend yields did not get sufficiently low to indicate a truly washed-out market. At the 1966 low, the Dow Jones Industrial Average was only yielding 4 percent; at the 1970 low, only 5 percent. That's a far cry from the 6½ percent yield of the 1974 bottom. Hence, yield proved a very useful tool for analyzing value during the 1966–1974 period.

Yield analysis was also especially valuable at the beginning of the 1949–1966 bull market. Between 1949 and 1953, during which time the DJIA recorded only one-sixth of its entire bull-market move, dividend yields on the DJIA were above 6 percent (see Figure 8-5.) In retrospect, stocks represented an outstanding value at that time.

Be sure not to limit your perspective to the stock market only. You should look all around, especially at competing forms of

FIGURE 8-4
(Courtesy of M. C. Horsey & Co.)

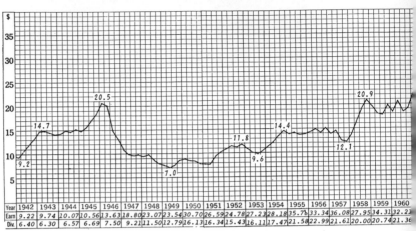

Year	1942	1943	1944	1945	1946	1947	1948	1949	1950	1951	1952	1953	1954	1955	1956	1957	1958	1959	1960
Earn	9.22	9.74	10.07	10.56	13.63	18.80	23.07	23.54	30.70	26.59	24.78	27.23	28.18	35.78	33.34	36.08	27.95	34.31	32.21
Div.	6.40	6.30	6.57	6.69	7.50	9.21	11.50	12.79	16.13	16.34	15.43	16.11	17.47	21.58	22.99	21.61	20.00	20.74	21.36

investment, such as bonds. As you can see from Figure 8-6, the spread between stock and bond yields is higher than at any time in the last 100 years. What's more, long-term interest rates are at their highest levels in almost 200 years. (See Figure 8-7.) That means, in effect, that bonds are more competitive with stocks than at any time during that period. It is important to be aware of bond yields because bonds can siphon away a lot of money that might normally go into the stock market. In fact, when bonds yield much more than stocks, they are usually a better investment. Some analysts believe a sustainable bull market won't begin until stocks yield more than bonds. As you can see from Figure 8-8, the spread between stocks and bonds reached 4.69 percent in favor of bonds during 1976—hardly a good omen for stocks.

There's one other important aspect of value which should be mentioned, and that's the quality of earnings. If earnings are overstated, then price/earnings ratios and dividend payout ratios are understated. Some analysts believe that the price/earnings ratio of the DJIA has been understated in recent years. Based on

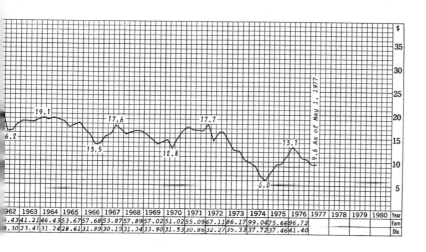

Year	1962	1963	1964	1965	1966	1967	1968	1969	1970	1971	1972	1973	1974	1975	1976	1977	1978	1979	1980
Earn	.43	41.21	46.43	53.67	57.68	53.87	57.89	57.02	51.02	55.09	67.11	86.17	99.04	75.66	96.72				
Div.	.30	23.41	31.24	28.61	31.89	30.19	31.34	33.90	31.53	30.86	32.27	35.33	37.72	37.46	41.40				

FIGURE 8-5

(Courtesy of Ian McAvity, *Deliberations*, Box 182, Adelaide St. Station, Toronto)

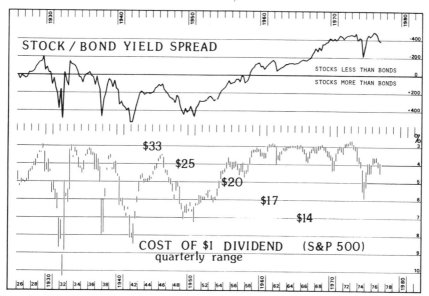

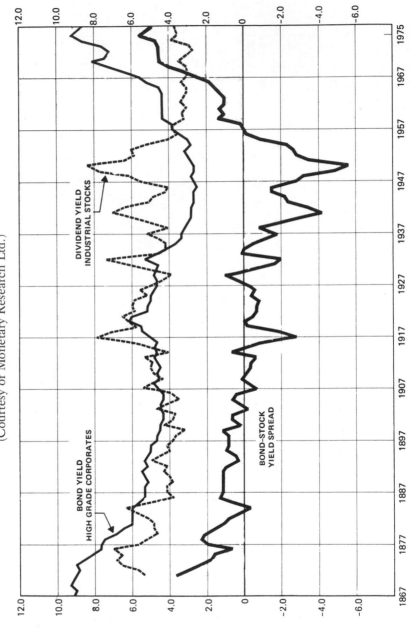

FIGURE 8-6
Historical Bond–Stock Yield Spread, 1867–1976
(Courtesy of Monetary Research Ltd.)

DIVIDEND YIELD
INDUSTRIAL STOCKS

BOND YIELD
HIGH GRADE CORPORATES

BOND–STOCK
YIELD SPREAD

FIGURE 8-7
(Courtesy of Salomon Brothers)

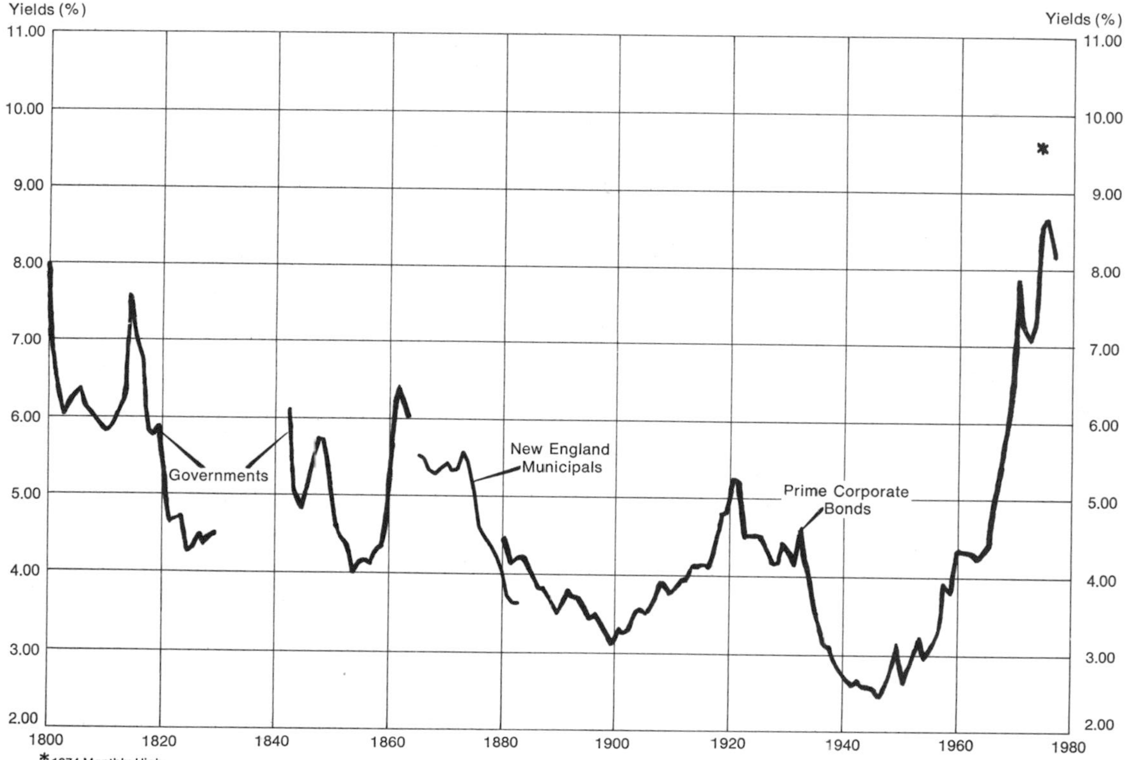

Yields (%)
11.00
10.00
9.00
8.00
7.00
6.00
5.00
4.00
3.00
2.00
Yields (%)
1800
1820
1840
1860
1880
1900
1920
1940
1960
1980
Governments
New England Municipals
Prime Corporate Bonds
*

*1974 Monthly High

FIGURE 8-8

(Courtesy of Ian McAvity, *Deliberations*, Box 182, Adelaide St. Station, Toronto)

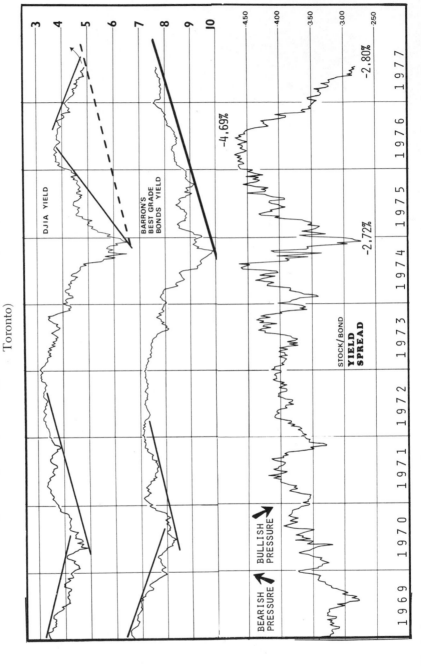

106

unfunded pension liabilities and replacement cost earnings, these analysts maintain that price/earnings are currently much higher than they seem.

If you decide, based on an analysis of dividend yield, book values, price/earnings ratios, dividend payout ratios, and competition from bonds, that the stock market is an unusual bargain, it then becomes a question of which stocks to buy. The first place to

FIGURE 8-9

(Courtesy of M. C. Horsey & Co.)

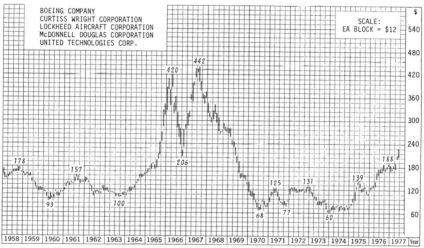

look is at those industry groups which have had a severe washout and are totally neglected. This is where investor expectations will be lowest and, hence, values will be greatest.

Ideally, you want a group which fulfills a long-term need and provides a necessary function or service. You'll want to make sure all the bad news on the group is out. Also be sure that a long period of base building has taken place. As you can see from Figure 8-9, aircraft and aerospace stocks had a big runup in the mid-1960s, then plummeted as the space program was nearing its peak and the protest against the Vietnam war built up. Then followed a double bottom over the course of a year, and finally a three-year period of base building. The time to buy the stocks, as you can see, was during that base-building period. The defense industry has its ups and downs, but it is not about to become obsolete. Not, at least, before the millenium.

It is not as hard as you may think to select one company out of an industry that has had some difficult times. Simply compare the earnings performances of all the companies in the industry during the bad times, and find out which one had the best record. Try to find out why it did better than the others. So long as it wasn't a fluke or a one-time affair, you should find out a lot about the capabilities of its management. After all, if the company does well when times are tough, won't it do spectacularly well when times are good?

Once you have selected the company you like, it is worth while to put it and the entire industry in perspective. The first step should be to determine what the entire company is valued at in the marketplace. To do this, take the number of shares the company has outstanding, and multiply that by the price of the stock. That will give you the total value which the market is ascribing to your company. Next do some comparisons. How does the total value of this company compare with other similar companies in the same business?

Now prepare a spread sheet for all the companies of a comparable nature in the industry. (If you don't know them all, ask your broker to prepare a list for you.) Then get at least five to six years of corporate data. Spread the results across a sheet of paper so that you can analyze the results.

Figure 8-10 shows what the spread sheet should look like. When you're finished, it should tell you a lot about your company's position in the industry. If you still feel that your company is the best value in the industry, then you can feel confident that you are buying a properly valued company.

108

Once you have selected the stock that you are interested in buying, whether it is a washed-out stock or not, it is important to understand how the stock trades. Like human beings, most stocks are different and have unusual characteristics. There may be quick-shooting market traders who go in and out of a stock; there may be banks and institutions who will support the stock; or it may be a purely retail-oriented stock, without organized sponsorship. In any event, watch the stock trade every day for months. See where it has support and where it meets resistance. At the very least, get a long-term chart of the stock.

Needless to say, it is very unwise to buy a stock you like when everyone else is rushing after it. An example is the uranium stocks which took off in a frantic rally after the antinuclear-power referendum was defeated in the June 8, 1976, primary vote in California. Atlas Corporation, a speculative uranium company, jumped from about 4½ to 7½ (on a presplit basis) in a matter of weeks. The stock was one of the most actively traded stocks on the New York Stock Exchange day after day, for several weeks. United Nuclear, a less speculative (and more of an investment-grade) issue, rose from about 24 to 40 in a like amount of time, also in a heavily traded environment. If investors had bought before the referendum, and before the stocks took off, they would have done well. But had they waited until after the referendum, they would have bought in a frenzied market environment. Only a few months later, investors could have bought United Nuclear as low as 27, and they could have bought Atlas as low as 3⅜.

And so it goes. There will always be another opportunity to buy the stock you want, so wait until the fundamentals are apparently weakening (which always will happen.) At such times, there will be more sellers than buyers, and you will have a good opportunity to pick up the stock at a very good price.

FIGURE 8-10
Sample Spread Sheet

	Company X	Company Y	Company Z

I. MARKET & DIVIDEND DATA

Where stock trades:
Current price:
Price range
    1977
    1976
    1975
    1974
    1973
    1972
Current P/E
P/E range
    1977
    1976
    1975
    1974
    1973
    1972
Indicated annual dividend rate = yield (%):
Last time dividend raised:
Last time equity was sold:

Status of insider transactions
over last 2 years (buying or selling
& amounts involved:)

Dividend payout as % of earnings
    1977
    1976
    1975
    1974
    1973
    1972

II. SALES & EARNINGS DATA

Net sales
    1977
    1976
    1975
    1974
    1973
    1972

Net earnings after taxes
    1977
    1976
    1975
    1974
    1973
    1972

Earnings per share
    1977
    1976
    1975
    1974
    1973
    1972

110

	Company X	Company Y	Company Z

Net profit margin
  1977
  1976
  1975
  1974
  1973
  1972

III. BALANCE-SHEET DATA

Common shares outstanding
Long-term debt
Stockholders' equity per share
Off-balance-sheet liabilities

IV. SHAREHOLDER DATA

Total value of company (number of shares
× price)
P/E relative to S&P 500
P/E relative to industry
Dividend yield relative to DJIA
Dividend yield relative to industry
Return on shareholders' equity
  1977
  1976
  1975
  1974
  1973
  1972

Annual compound rate of return on
equity for last 5 years

Annual compound growth rate in earnings per share for last 5 years

Dividend yield compared to bonds

V. CORPORATE DATA

% of market share your company has
  1977
  1976
  1975
  1974
  1973
  1972

- New products about to be launched:
- What is the importance of new products
  to the company?
- Is your company getting competition
  from other businesses?
- Are there any unjustified expectations in the stock?

111

9

Value is in Timing

Don't tell me what to buy, tell me when to buy it.

JOHN MAGEE

Market timing, or the time at which you buy or sell stocks, is critical to investment success. It is important because it can have a substantial impact on the amount of money that you get for a stock when you sell it or how much a stock costs when you buy it. For some strange reason, we are much more price-conscious as consumers than we are as investors. In late 1974, consumers in general did not want to buy automobiles for a variety of reasons, but price was certainly a major consideration. When General Motors, Ford, and Chrysler offered a cash rebate on new cars in early 1975, consumers flocked to the showrooms, thereby indicating how sensitive they were to price. If only investors applied this same consciousness of price to the stock market, there would be fewer investment losses.

As we mentioned in an earlier chapter, there are several types of market timing. There is the selling which should be done at the ultimate top of a bull market. There is also the possible selling which could be done at one of the various phases or legs of a bull market, at the end of which there is invariably a sharp reaction.

And there is the buying and selling of individual stocks, irrespective of the direction of the market.

It is acknowledged in some quarters that bull markets have three upward steps or legs. The professional investor buys stocks on the first wave or leg, the business person buys on the second wave or leg, and the public buys on the third wave. According to this theory, it is not wise to expect more than three legs during any bull move, although one should always be prepared for a fourth leg.

Bear markets can also have three downward steps. The reasoning here is that the most timid investors sell during the first step downward, and so on, until the most tenacious investor finally lets go near the bottom. It is interesting to note that in the aftermath of the 1949–1966 bull market, the decline took place in three stages. There were the 1966 decline to 744, the 1970 drop to 631, and the plunge to 578 in 1974. (See Figure 9-1.)

FIGURE 9-1
Three Downward Steps

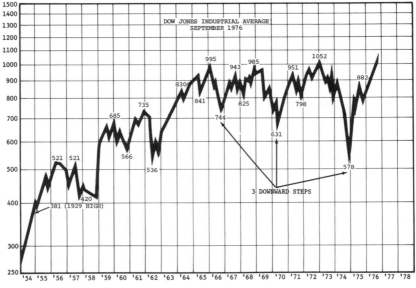

Some analysts don't attach much credence to "legs." They prefer to divide a bull market into three phases. The first phase of the bull market sees stock prices rise back to a reasonable valuation—not a *proper* valuation, but a reasonable one. The fire-sale prices of the previous decline are no longer around. The second phase is when stocks go up in response to an improving business environment: earnings are jumping and dividends are being increased. During the third phase, which is where the public comes in, stock prices rise above their intrinsic value and begin to discount future events (which may or may not come to pass). No matter how one looks at the market—in phases or legs—market timing can be useful.

It would have paid investors well to have gotten out of the stock market at the end of the great 1949–1966 bull market. If investors then put their funds into short-term treasury bills or some other liquid money-market instrument, they would have outperformed all but a few investment advisors.

There are three basic tools which investors can use to select the time to buy and sell stocks: economic, monetary, and psychological. The economic indicators are the ones that are concerned with the outlook for business. If the economy is growing in real terms, sooner or later corporate profits and dividends will grow too—which is bullish for stock prices. (The reverse is also true. A recession or a decline in real gross national product poses the threat of declining corporate profits and dividend cuts.) The monetary indicators deal primarily with action of the Federal Reserve and the demand for credit. They measure, among other things, the outlook for long-term interest rates—which is especially important because bond yields are often competitive with stock yields. The psychological or sentiment indicators are the ones that deal with investors' attitudes to stocks. They attempt to gauge (1) whether stocks are in strong or weak hands, (2) the amount of potential buying power available to come into the market, (3) whether selling pressure has dried up, and (4) if the market is under the influence of the crowd and is behaving emotionally.

The economic indicators, which measure the state of the economy, can be employed to confirm the direction of stock prices. If the economy is growing at an unsustainable pace, chances are that stock prices will soon start to concentrate on the economic weakness which must surely follow. Likewise, if the economy is contracting at an unsustainable rate, stock prices will soon begin to reflect the better business environment which will follow. The state of the economy can also be used to see whether the stock market has fully discounted the best or worst that can happen. For example, during the fall of 1976, many commentators feared that economic growth was slowing and that the economy was about to enter a recession.

There was some substantiation for their fears in the economic news of that time: Leading economic indicators for August and September fell, and the October figures were flat. (Three successive declines in the leading economic indicators is regarded by some as a signal that the economy is headed toward recession.) Retail sales were flat to down; demand for steel dropped sharply (and a steel price increase had to be rescinded); automobile sales were running below the year-ago levels; the rest of the industrialized nations were in even more trouble than the United States.

The stock market reacted badly to the first piece of poor economic news to come out: On the day on which the decline in leading economic indicators for August was announced, the Dow Jones Industrial Average plunged nearly 20 points. From that point on, the average dropped some 100 points in a little more than two weeks. But after that, the DJIA traded in a narrow range in the 925 area while more and more bad economic news came out. The longer this holding pattern lasted, the more apparent it

116

became that the stock market was not reacting to the bad news anymore. By November, the Dow Jones Industrial Average started rallying, and it eventually reached 1000 by the end of the year.

This is how the economic indicators or economic developments can be used to predict future market action. In other words, the economy had slowed down, and the stock market had anticipated it. When the actual event occurred, all the people who were going to sell stocks at that time had already done so.

The credit or monetary indicators are even more useful. For one thing, they are often the earliest in giving a signal. That's because credit is such an important part of our economy. So, in the autumn of 1974, the first sign of recession was a lessening in the demand for credit. As a result, the monetary indicators turned favorable and gave a clue that the long decline in stock prices might soon be over.

The same is true at market tops. If credit demands are excessive (because of inventory or stock speculation), the economy and, by inference, corporate profits face some large risks. First, the Federal Reserve will probably tighten credit, which sooner or later will affect the business outlook. Second, intense inventory or stock speculation cannot go on forever. Thus, when it ends (as it always does), the aftermath may be severe.

The best monetary indicators are the Dow Jones twenty-bond index, the Dow Jones Utility Average, and the NYSE Utility Average. Utilities and bonds are yield instruments and thus are money-sensitive and influenced by interest rates.

Certain long-term government bonds are also a good early lead indicator of the market. (Government bonds are often the first to react to changing credit conditions. At the end of a decline in bonds, traders generally seek out quality first. Thus government bonds are among the first to move upward. And when economic conditions and credit demands get very robust, banks tend to sell government issues to free up funds for loans.) The monetary indicators certainly worked at the bottom of the market in 1974. The Dow Jones Utility Average, which had been declining since 1965, bottomed at 57 in September 1974, some three weeks before the Dow Jones Industrial Average did. (If you consider the real bottom as taking place in December 1974, the Utilities bottomed 2½ months before the DJIA.) Then the Utility Average rose sharply throughout the rest of the year, forecasting the subsequent advance in stock prices which began in January 1975.

The bond market, as represented by the Dow Jones Twenty-bond average, also pointed to an easing of credit conditions and a bottom in stocks in 1974. It bottomed in August 1974 and rallied substantially throughout the fall and into 1975.

The monetary or credit indicators also worked well in predicting the large market advance in early 1976. Here again the monetary indicators were active and pointing higher well before the market took off. The Dow Jones Utility Average and twenty-bond average had been strong for several weeks prior to the breakout of the Industrials into new high ground.

There are basically three significant sentiment (or psychological) indicators. (These are a way of measuring how much emotion is in the market. If a lot of emotion is influencing people's judgment, the market is behaving irrationally and stocks are close to an extreme point where a reversal of trend occurs.)

First among the sentiment indicators is the New York Stock Exchange specialist short-sales ratio. (Specialists, in effect, "make the market" in stocks that are traded on the floor of the exchange. Their function is to maintain an orderly market in the stocks they represent; in doing so, they can buy or sell short the stock to any degree that is necessary. Because of their intimate knowledge of the stock—how it trades and its supply/demand situation—specialists are in a strong position to assess the risk/reward ratio of being either short or long. The financial survival of specialists dictates that they be right most of the time; otherwise they will quickly lose their capital and be forced out of the business.) The raw data on specialists are released at the end of every week by the New York Stock Exchange and can be obtained from *Barron's* or the *Wall Street Journal* on Monday mornings.

The ratio is computed by dividing the total volume of short sales for the week into the total volume of specialist short sales. (See Figure 9-2.) The parameters of the ratio are 40 percent and

FIGURE 9-2
Specialist and Member Short-Sales Ratios

Each week, the data on specialist and member short sales are printed in the *Wall Street Journal* and certain other major financial publications. (Note that the figures are released with a two-week lag.) These figures can be found in the *Wall Street Journal* every Monday morning on one of the last few pages. Here's an example of the way the statement usually appears:

	Purchases	Sales (including short sales)	Short sales
Total:	94,795,520	94,795,520	6,800,290
For member accounts:			
As specialists	10,140,050	10,644,470	3,053,670
As floor traders	315,000	345,900	66,900
Others (except as odd lot dealers)	10,758,287	12,016,015	2,636,260

To compute the NYSE specialist short sales ratio, take the figures for specialist short sales and divide that by the total number of short sales. In this example, you'd take 3,053,670 and divide it by 6,800,290—which would give you a ratio of 44.8 percent.

To compute the NYSE member short sales ratio, add up all of the short sales of the various member accounts and divide that by the total number of short sales. In this case, you'd add together 3,053,670, 66,900, and 2,636,260 and divide that by 6,800,290. The result would be a member short ratio of 84.6 percent.

65 percent. Anything under 40 percent is bullish; anything over 65 percent is bearish. The rationale behind this is that when specialists reduce their short position to 40 percent or less of total short sales, they're betting that a rally will take place in the near future. At the bottom of the bear market in the fall of 1974, the specialist short-sales ratio fell below 40 percent for many weeks in succession. Likewise, at the top in 1973, the ratio gave an early warning signal by rising above 65 percent and staying there. (Note that if you compute the figures based on a four-week moving average, which is a good idea, the bearish/bullish parameters are 58 percent and 42 percent, respectively. See Figure 9-3.)

This indicator is not necessarily precise and must be judged along with other measures of sentiment, such as the member short-sales ratio, odd-lot short sales, and your general feel of what most investors think about the market.

The member short-sales ratio is similar to the specialist short-sales ratio in that it registers the short-selling activity of all members of the New York Stock Exchange (which includes almost every brokerage firm dealing in stocks). See Figure 9-2.

Like the specialist, the members of the NYSE have a good insight into what's going on. They know (in a general sense) what the institutions and banks are doing, how much stock is overhanging the market, etc. Hence, when they reduce their short positions to 70 percent or less of the total short position, that's a bullish sign. A ratio above 85 percent is considered bearish. This ratio has shown good results in calling various turns, but it is far from infallible.

The odd-lot short-sales ratio is somewhat distorted these days because so many stocks are selling below 20. Thus, odd-lot orders are much less frequent than they were in the past. What's more, the options market has siphoned away a lot of the players who might formerly have participated in odd-lot transactions. Hence,

FIGURE 9-3

(Courtesy Ian McAvity, *Deliberations*, Box 182, Adelaide St. Station, Toronto)

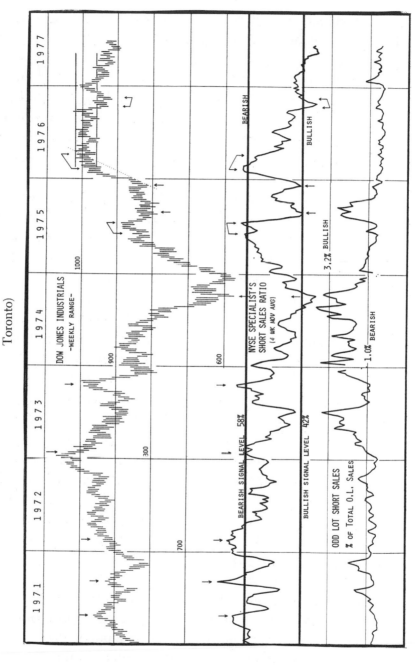

the old odd-lot parameters may not apply. All the same, this ratio is worth watching, as a confirmation of what's happening elsewhere.

Formerly, odd-lot short sales as a percentage of odd-lot sales would have had to rise to above 3 percent to be truly bullish, and fall below 1 percent to be bearish. Even if that figure isn't reached, when the odd-lot short-sales ratio suddenly jumps to the highest level in a year and climbs from 0.5 percent to 1½ percent, you should start to take note.

Why is the odd-lot short-sales ratio a good barometer of sentiment? It seems that odd-lot short sellers are the Wrong-Way Corrigans of Wall Street. At major turning points, they are always wrong: They become overly optimistic (and are afraid to short) near tops, and they short heavily near market bottoms.

Be sure not to use these indicators in a black-and-white fashion. For instance, at times during 1977, the specialist short-sales ratio was bullish, while the member short-sales ratio and odd lot short sales were bearish. Anyone who had relied solely on the specialist short-sales ratio would have gotten into trouble.

Economic, monetary, and psychological indicators can also be used to point to an intermediate "correction" in stocks. It should be noted, however, that intermediate corrections are difficult to call. That is because they take place within the overall confines of a bull market (or a rally in a bear market) and therefore tend to go against the primary trend. A correction within a primary trend can have very little to do with the actual underlying fundamentals. It can result from profit taking or the apparent fear on the part of many investors that some bad economic event may take place.

A good case in point is the correction which took place after the first leg up after the 1974 bottom. The Dow Jones Industrial Average advanced very sharply between January 1975 and July 1975 (when it topped out at 880). At that time, commodity prices were heading up, the Federal Reserve was squeezing credit, and interest rates were heading higher. The market went into a sharp tailspin and declined to around 780, bouncing off that level once in August and again in October.

However, the jump in commodities was caused mainly by the Russian grain deal and the psychological effect that had on speculators (who remembered the 1972 Russian grain deal and the resultant jump in commodity prices). The Fed also had to tighten up because the rebates of the 1975 stimulus program were coming into the economy and the money supply threatened to bulge. Neither of those two events was long-lasting, and the Federal Reserve was able to ease up by the fall of 1975. As soon as it did, the monetary indicators improved and the stock market subsequently took off in the last weeks of 1975.

It is very important to remember that a correction in a bull market or a rally in a bear market is much more convincing than the real thing. For example, the bear-market rally of late 1973 was one of the strongest-looking markets of all time. The DJIA rallied from around 850 to 1000 in a period of two months, accompanied by large volume and widely bullish sentiment.

This fits well with the premise that the stock market does what it can to confound the greatest number of investors. If we're in a bear market, the goal of the market is to fall as low as possible before investors start to get out. Periodically, the market must have euphoric rallies which will suck back in, at high prices, any money that has managed to escape. In bull markets, the reverse is true. The stock market's goal is to get as high as it can with as few investors participating as possible. Savage, frightening corrections appear from time to time to shake out the weak holders, thus forcing them to buy back later at much higher prices.

Take June and August 1974 as examples of a deceptive bear-market rally. The DJIA rallied some 65 points in 5 days in early June 1974, terrifying the short sellers and giving renewed confi-

123

dence to the bulls. Subsequently, just before President Nixon resigned, there was massive speculation that his resignation would be bullish for the stock market. A rally took place, and the Dow Jones Industrial Average rose from about 750 to a little above 800, in a matter of two to three days. This again was a period during which optimism was widespread and everyone was convinced that a 150-point rally was in the offing. The truth was something different, however. The sharpest decline in years was in the offing; the DJIA plunged from 800 to the high 500s without a rally of consequence.

10

Let the Market Averages Do the Talking

Descartes tried to learn about the world he lived in by assuming that he knew nothing except that he was a thinking being. Only after he had eliminated all the other assumptions would he start to build toward conclusions on anything. How many times have you noticed that crime investigators are misled because they assume too much? Their confusion comes from the fact that they made one wrong assumption; as a result, all the rest of their conclusions are wrong.

In the 1920s, a young scientist discovered how to make a radio small enough to fit into a car. This man had never been to college, so he'd never read the famous dissertation, by an eminent scientist, which effectively proved that a small radio couldn't be built. Since this young man had never seen the dissertation, he was not misled by its false assumptions.

How then can we eliminate emotions and assumptions from the stock market? The first way is to let the Averages do all the talking. One successful market forecaster has found it to be the single most effective market tool over the years. It was largely responsible, he says, for enabling him to catch the 1974 bottom. At that time, the analyst said: "I'm going to get rid of all my emotions about the economy, the fear of a credit collapse, and

I'm going to watch the market. If I see examples that most, or all of the selling is over with, and if the Averages confirm that, then I'm going to buy some stocks." As it turned out, the Averages told the real story.

The first measure of the Averages is what is called the Dow Theory or Dow's Theory, after Charles Dow, the founder of the *Wall Street Journal.* The basic rationale behind Dow's Theory is the interaction of the Dow Jones Industrial Average with the Dow Jones Transporation Average. The Industrials represent the manufacturing capacity of the nation; the Transports represent the selling or shipping capacity. There's a very basic relationship between those two areas, and if one gets out of whack with the other, trouble results.

In other words, if the Industrial Average is doing better than the Transportation Average, more goods are being produced than shipped. More goods being produced than transported implies that inventory hoarding is going on. What happens when inventory hoarding stops? You have a major recession, as you did in 1974–1975, or you have a period of slow growth, as you did in the latter part of 1976.

On the other hand, if more goods are being transported than produced, inventories may soon run low. And when that happens, everyone may get on the bandwagon at once and start producing more goods—which poses the danger of bottlenecks and lost sales due to the unavailability of goods.

In summation, the economy is a machine, and if there are imbalances in any areas, there will be problems. The Averages try to measure these imbalances and anticipate them. According to the Dow Theory, both Averages must confirm each other by penetrating preceding high or low points. Note the emphasis on both Averages: A new high or new low in one average is almost always misleading and deceptive. Thus, practitioners of the Dow Theory are always looking for what they call nonconfirmations.

The Averages were successful in calling the end of the bull market in 1966, the last time both Averages reached a new all-time high together. (Even though the market became highly speculative in 1968, the DJIA didn't go to a new high.) Although the Industrials went to a new all-time high of 1051 in January 1973, that move was unconfirmed by the Transports, which peaked out almost a year earlier without going to a new all-time high. (See Figure 10-1.)

There is no time requirement, during which one average must confirm the other, but the longer the amount of time that elapses between a high in one average and a confirmation by the other average, the greater the cause for concern.

The confirmation principle is especially useful at turning points and in helping to separate the spurious from the real. The action of one average can often be very misleading. As a result, investors can often be fooled into thinking that the market is headed lower when, in reality, it's about to head up, and vice versa.

Another interesting point to remember is that a signal of a change in trend is considered good until there's a definite signal that the trend has been reversed. This should help keep investors out of bear-market rallies and keep them from selling at the wrong time in bull-market advances.

It is important to remember, however, that the Dow Theory is not precise. Frequently, a good portion of a bull move has already taken place before a signal is given. But what is wrong with that? If we have to give up a little in order to reduce risks, that is a worthy trade-off.

One other point about the Dow Theory bears mentioning. It has called a number of tops and bottoms in recent years, and as a result, is now a widely followed indicator. This popularity means it may not be as useful in the immediate future as it has been in the recent past.

FIGURE 10-1(a)
Dow Jones Industrial Average
(Courtesy of M. C. Horsey & Co.)

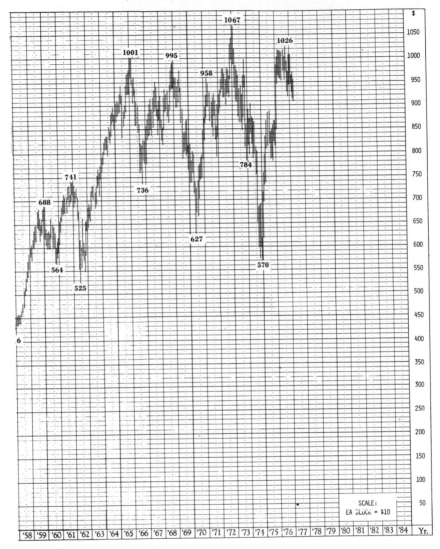

128

FIGURE 10-1(b)
Dow Jones Transportation Average
(Courtesy of M. C. Horsey & Co.)

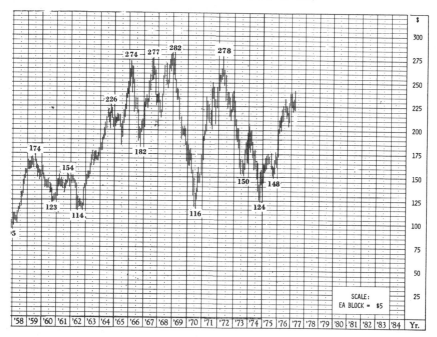

Next on the list of the Averages is what's called the *confirmation indicators*. These are used as a means of determining the true direction of the market. The Dow Jones Industrial Average, the "market" to most people, can frequently be very misleading (and at the worst of times). In late 1972 and early 1973, just prior to the end of the bull move, the DJIA rose to a new all-time high of 1067, amid much fanfare that the 1000 mark had finally been broken. In truth, however, the average stock was behaving poorly, and it was only a few stocks in the DJIA, such as Eastman Kodak and Procter & Gamble, that took the average up.

The Dow Jones Industrial Average was also misleading at the bottom in December 1974. The Industrials had a closing low of 584 in October 1974, then rallied 100 points and fell to a new closing low in December of 570. To the casual observer, the Dow

FIGURE 10-2
Dow Jones 30 Industrials
(Courtesy of William O'Neil & Co.)

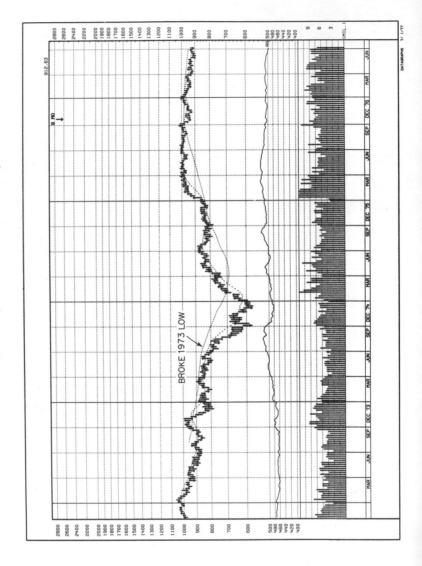

FIGURE 10-3
NYSE—Composite
(Courtesy of William O'Neil & Co.)

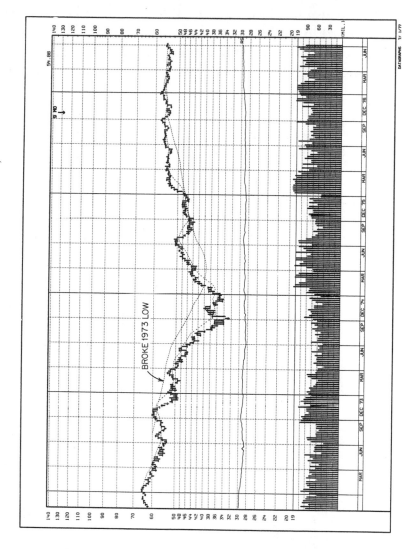

131

had broken its old low and was headed down, but in reality the selling and the bear market were over. (It might be worth noting, parenthetically, that the new low in the Industrials was not confirmed by a new low in the Transports. This was one reason why several analysts turned bullish at that time.)

Since the DJIA frequently sends off misleading signals, one must have other signposts to verify its direction. One of the simplest tools to use is the New York Stock Exchange Composite Index, a composite average of some 1500 stocks on the New York Stock Exchange, and hence a better proxy of the market than the

FIGURE 10-4
Dow Jones Industrial Average and Stock-Market Breadth
(Courtesy of Monetary Research, Ltd.)

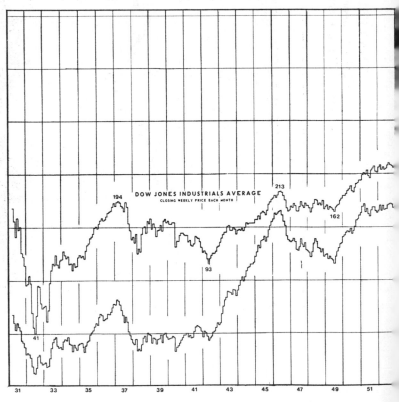

thirty Dow Industrials. Here too, check to see if previous high points and low points are confirmed by both averages. In 1974, for example, the NYSE Composite was very helpful. Although the DJIA didn't violate the 1973 lows until July 1974 (thereby confirming that the bear market was still on), the NYSE Composite broke its 1973 low early in the year. What's more, it kept falling during the whole period in which the DJIA's strength led some investors into a false complacency. (See Figures 10-2 and 10-3.)

The advance/decline ratio fulfills a similar function, although it requires a little more work. You take the daily difference between

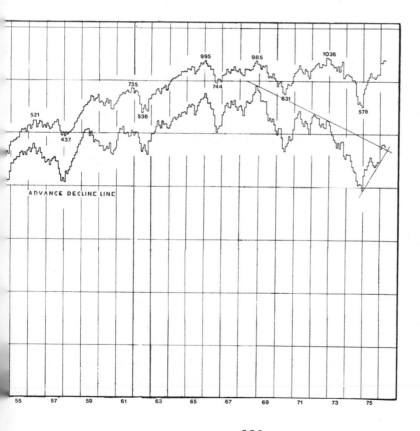

the number of advancing and declining issues on the New York Stock Exchange and divide it by the number of issues traded. Do this every day, and you'll have a running calculation of "market breadth," another way of measuring how "the market is doing." (The advance/decline ratio is almost a barometer for business activity as a whole. If an economic advance is to be sustainable, it must include as many sectors of the economy as possible. An economic environment in which only a few growth stocks, or only the thirty Industrials, prosper is not a healthy one.) Ideally, you want to see each move by the Dow confirmed by the advance/decline ratio. So, a new recovery high in the Dow should also have a new recovery high in the advance/decline ratio. See how each new high in the DJIA was confirmed by a new high in the weekly advance/decline ratio in Figure 10-4.

The daily advance/decline ratio was particularly useful at the 1974 bottom. After a collapse of close to five years, the ratio began to improve as early as October and held its ground in the December pullback of the Dow Jones Industrial Average. And then the advance/decline ratio rose throughout most of 1975–1976.

Another confirmation indicator is the *London Financial Times Index*. This Index has frequently made a turn well before the United States stock market. For instance, the London market topped out in January 1929, nearly nine months before ours. Similarily, the London market bottomed in June 1932, about a month before our bear market ended. More recently, the London market peaked about six months before the DJIA did in January 1973.

Basically, then, we can remove some of the disadvantages we face in the stock market if we let the averages and the market itself do the talking. At certain times, it is well worth forgetting our own preconceived opinions in order to objectively evaluate what the market is telling us. For instance, in September 1976, the Dow Jones Industrial Average failed to better its all-time high by only a small margin. Then, a few months later, the year-end rally failed to better the September high. Both of these failures were warning signals that choppy water might lie ahead for investors. That was true irrespective of the level of earnings and dividends, price/earnings ratios, price to book value, price/dividend ratios, the trend of interest rates, and the outlook for the economy. The Dow Jones Industrial Average had every opportunity to hit a new all-time high, but that was not to be. The Dow Jones Industrial Average had spoken loud and clear, and the best policy at the time was to listen to its message.

11

Philosophy Transcends Emotion

All the theories in the world come to naught unless they work. The psychiatrist who understands human emotions to the nth degree is a failure unless patients benefit from that understanding. A revolutionary economic theory is worthless unless it's practical. Likewise, investment theory serves no purpose unless it can help investors make money (and keep what they make).

Mistakes in the stock market, as elsewhere, most frequently occur when there is no underlying philosophy, no long-term goal and plan of action. By philosophy and plan of action we mean a discipline, a set of rules which are vigorously enforced, a time-proven conceptual approach, and a consistency of method. Only in this way can investing be successful.

Picking the right investment philosophy has a lot to do with the particular emotional makeup of the individual. Is he a man of action? Is she a woman of thought? Does he or she have patience? Does she like to look at things close up or in panorama? Of course, knowledge, experience, amount of capital, desire for risk and gains, and time available for investing are also key factors. But the type of person you are is the critical element in developing an investment philosophy.

Some people are extremely active and high strung and simply aren't able to buy a stock and hold on to it. For these people, a long-term investment strategy is difficult to embrace—even though at times it gets the best results. One way to be "active" and invest for the long term is to concentrate 95 percent of your funds on long-term investments, and the rest in highly volatile, speculative situations, such as options or low-priced stocks. This is a way of satisfying the need to be always doing something. You can trade in and out of the options or low-priced stocks as much as you want and still have a philosophy which works.

There is no dearth of investment philosophies; college professors and whiz kids are constantly coming up with new ways to "beat the market." But do they work? And should anyone ever try a new scheme until time and perspective have a go at deflating it? Would you, after all, try a new miracle drug before it's been tested? Certainly not! And therefore an investment philosophy or strategy should only be adopted if it has passed the test of time.

In this chapter, we briefly discuss some rather unusual investment philosophies which have worked and continue to work. They are employed by some of Wall Street's most astute and successful money managers. Perhaps you will find one that particularly appeals to you.

All these strategies try to reduce, as much as possible, the challenge which faces any investor in the stock market. They seek to minimize assumptions, quantify extreme emotions, and reduce risks wherever possible. They can be broken down into four main categories. The first is what we must call the strategy of adversity—a philosophy which concentrates on the major economic problems of the day and the companies or industries that can solve these problems. The second is the pure search for an undervalued stock. This value is arrived at by the simplest and most basic method: If the corporation were to be liquidated today, would its liquidating value per share be significantly more than the present stock price?

The third strategy, which is a variation on the second, attempts to locate companies whose fortunes have had a bad reversal and whose stock price has already discounted the worst that can happen. The fourth is the strategy of buying a stock (or stocks) only at those moments when fear dominates the market.

THE PHILOSOPHY OF ADVERSITY

No investors would have stock-market losses if they could accurately predict the future. This is, after all, what speculation or investing is all about. You buy something today with the expectation that it will be more valuable (and more sought after) tomorrow. If you know what tomorrow will bring, your chances of going wrong are virtually eliminated.

Precisely because we have no second sight, our expectations of future events frequently don't work out. But we can get a small glimpse of the future through the looking glass of adversity. It is in the nature of humans to want to solve problems. The problems are not always soluble; nor do we always focus on the important ones. Nevertheless, the more dramatic and overwhelming the problem is, the surer we can be that people on all sides will unite together to deal with it.

So it was that the great depression and devastating deflation of the 1930s was eventually cured. The rebuilding of Europe after the Second World War and the war on poverty and racial injustice are other examples of problems which caught the imagination of the people.

No one can be precise about predicting when a country will mobilize itself to solve a problem. However, one can generally state that the longer the problem is allowed to continue, and the more serious it becomes, the better the chances are that something will have to be done about it.

Investing in a company (or companies) which have or are developing the capability to solve problems or will benefit from their solution is a relatively safe way of predicting the future. Of course, you must make sure of three things: (1) The adversity must be very real. (2) Support for dealing with it must be growing. (3) The company you buy must get an economic benefit—higher sales and earnings—from these developments.

Let us look at some problems we face today. There is, first, the shortage of energy, a crisis that is finally coming home to people. This energy crisis will unquestionably get worse before it gets better. And companies that can provide economic sources of energy, such as nuclear power, are in position to do well in the years ahead.

A good time to have invested in certain small, unknown energy companies was in 1975, or even early 1976. By then, the Arab oil embargo and the previous energy-crisis fanfare were long forgotten. Consumers were right back to their old consumption habits, and the impasse in finding new energy sources was at its height. Domestic natural-gas and oil prices were held way below their replacement costs; environmentalists were attempting to eliminate nuclear power; and the mining of western coal was held up by uncertainties concerning strip mining.

In other words, you should employ the adversity strategy only when the adversity is apparently forgotten or not recognized by the majority. If you have done your homework, and the problem is long-lasting and of a profound nature, it will keep coming back to haunt the nation until something is done about it.

The huge migration to the sunbelt is another potentially interesting investment possibility. You could take advantage of this population shift by investing in a consumer company which operates exclusively in the South, such as a Texas retail chain. Alternatively, investors could key their strategy to what Congress is likely to do to stem the population flow. At least initially, Congress may well fund the improvement of northeastern ports and spend some money on Conrail in an attempt to rejuvenate the bankrupt northeast rail system. No matter how you look at it,

140

something must be done to mend the declining economic fortunes of the northeast.

THE PHILOSOPHY OF VALUE

This strategy requires that you look at a stock as if you were a corporate purchaser interested in buying the entire company. The best way to figure out what a company is really worth is by calculating what's called "net current assets per share." This figure is found by subtracting all liabilities (including long-term lease obligations and unfunded pension liabilities) from the current assets and dividing the difference by the total number of shares outstanding. If the value of the company is 30 percent to 60 percent higher than the current price of the stock, it's probably a good candidate for purchase.

Note that diversification is extremely important to this strategy. A typical $50,000 portfolio should be invested in twenty to thirty companies. That way, if anything goes wrong with one company, the loss will have only a minimal effect on the whole portfolio. Diversification also has the advantage of boosting investment results. You never know when the stock market will properly value your holdings—it might take three years or more. But the odds are great that one or two of the twenty to thirty stocks might be recognized soon.

Knowing when to sell is also a key part of this strategy. A good time to sell is when the stock's price approaches its net current assets per share. This enables you to get out of the stock market well before a bull-market top. If stocks are overpriced, which inevitably occurs at market tops, there won't be anything attractive to invest in. Selling when a company becomes properly valued also produces a constant source of new cash that can be invested in other attractive bargains. (It's unwise to sell one unrealized bargain just because a better bargain comes along.)

Of course, as a bull market progresses, there will be fewer and fewer stocks which represent value on a liquidation basis. That should be a meaningful signal to the investor who uses this approach. If stock prices reflect more than companies are worth, stocks are not a good buy; hence, the best move at this point is to sit on the sidelines until the next bear market.

THE PHILOSOPHY OF THE WASHED-OUT STOCK

As we've mentioned before, the place to look for value is in the stock or area which everyone else is ignoring. In other words, try to find a stock with strong underlying assets that is currently out of investor favor for one reason or another. The dividend may have been cut or a huge loss reported, or maybe a major write-off has taken place.

The first rule of this approach is to concentrate on stocks which are not highly visible. These are the stocks that have low investor expectations. That way, there aren't apt to be any disappointments. If the company unexpectedly reports a bad quarter or a foreign-currency loss, the stock shouldn't react much. In fact, if the stock is really washed out, it won't even be affected by bad news. After a certain period of time, investors become impervious to bad news. And all the shareholders who are going to sell at rock-bottom prices will have already done so. From there, the stock has nowhere to go but up.

Here are some of the characteristics of a washed-out stock:

- Trading becomes very inactive.

- Stock analysts stop visiting the company.

- No security analysts, market-letter writers, or financial reporters cover the company.

142

- The company's management has stopped selling stock and may even be buying some.

After you've found a washed-out stock, wait for some evidence of a fundamental turnaround before you decide to buy it. For example, the company might be selling off its unprofitable operations or liquidating assets—which could significantly improve the company's finances. A new management team or chief executive officer could be another tip-off of a turnaround. You should also watch insider trading activity very closely. If there's a lot of buying going on, something positive may be in the wind.

Keep track of any 13d statements that are filed with the Securities and Exchange Commission. (By law, any individual or company that owns more than 5 percent of a company's outstanding stock must file a 13d with the SEC.) If a new buyer has entered the picture, it could mean that a tender offer may be about to take place or that some investor or company sees a great value in the company's assets and is willing to put money on the line.

Another key area to watch is the minority position of a major shareholder. For example, if a major corporation owns 20 percent of a company which has just gotten into financial trouble, you can be fairly sure that the big company will do everything in its power to make its investment pay off.

THE PHILOSOPHY OF FEAR

The art of money management is basically that of managing cash—and waiting for an unusual opportunity to put it to work. These opportunities are most prevalent when the market is dominated by fear. At such times, as we've seen before, investors will throw away stocks, irrespective of intrinsic value.

Fear is generally created by a political or economic event.

(JFK's confrontation with the steel industry was an example of a political event; the 1974 decline in stock prices was an example of an economic one.) Fear can be measured by looking at the relationship of all the stocks on the New York Stock Exchange to each other. In a normal environment, most stocks act independently of each other; but when fear predominates, all stocks go down together. When you see such an event take place, you can assume that a buying opportunity may be near.

If fear is too intangible a quality for you to deal with, consider building up cash reserves until a recession occurs. Wait until the economic statistics show indisputably that we have entered a recession. The textbook definition of this is that real gross national product must decline for two consecutive quarters. Since the economic numbers are generally released well after the end of the quarter, you would probably learn about the recession two months or so after the end of the second quarter. If you had bought stocks at that time in the postwar period, your performance would have been excellent. In the twelve months following each such buy point, the Standard & Poor's 500 jumped 30 percent on average. (There were five such occasions.)

It is time to sell, according to this theory, when the economy starts to grow at an unsustainable rate. If the gross national product is booming at, say, a 10 percent annual rate for a quarter or two, you should become highly cautious. Such growth cannot be sustained for long. Hence, such events should be the signal to liquidate your portfolio of stocks. Then, simply wait for the next bear-induced decline.

12

How Contrary Opinion Can
Help You Be Objective

"Contrary opinion" is one of the best ways, perhaps the best way, to stay aloof from the psychology of the crowd. As we saw in previous chapters, the power of the crowd and the influence of the crowd on one's emotions can be the single most dangerous element in stock-market investing.

What is contrary opinion, and why does it deserve such praise? To summarize succinctly, contrary opinion is a theory by which one attempts to analyze and determine precisely what the popular opinion is, and then act contrary to it. This opinion must be widely held and it must be pervasive; otherwise the herd instinct is not in effect. But if it is, then the prevalent feeling must be one of emotion. And, as we've seen before, too much emotion restricts rational analysis.

Humphrey Neill, the father of the art of contrary thinking, describes it this way in his book, *The Art of Contrary Thinking* (Caxton, 1971): "The art of contrary thinking may be stated simply: Thrust your thoughts out of the rut. In a word, be a noncomformist when using your mind. Sameness of thinking is a natural attribute. So you must expect to practice . . . in order to get into the habit of throwing your mind into directions which are opposite to the obvious."

Contrary opinion is successful for several reasons. First, if the majority of individuals expect a certain event to occur, they will take the necessary action to prevent it from happening. For instance, since the economy bottomed in early 1975, many investors, economists, and business people feared that inflation would reignite once the economy began to accelerate. This view was widely publicized in all the major business and financial publications, and hardly a day went by without considerable attention being devoted to this point. The slightest jump in commodity prices, or increase in bank loans or interest rates, was viewed as the beginning of another period of overexpansion, soon to be followed by a period of tightening monetary policy and then recession. But because this view was so widely held and so publicized, business people, consumers, and investors remained inordinately cautious. Hence, their caution prevented any of the excesses that might have caused the event which they feared so much.

Take the first quarter of 1976 as an example. This quarter was characterized by unusually high economic growth, low inflation, and strong consumer spending. As soon as the excellent results of the first quarter were released, business and consumer confidence jumped. At the same time, business began to increase inventories, which in turn put upward pressures on commodity prices. At the very first sign of higher prices, consumers began to worry, and they cut back on spending. As a result, business people found themselves with excessive inventories, given the slower consumer sales. A period of slower inventory accumulation (and even some inventory liquidation) took place. For this reason, pressure on commodity prices soon diminished, and the rate of inflation remained under control. In other words, what everybody expected did not occur, simply because when it did begin to occur, they took action which prevented its continu-

146

ance. Humphrey Neill would explain the above phenomenon in this manner:

> A businessman is going to be impressed, when he picks up his newspaper or magazine, and sees that eighty, or two hundred, economists see eye to eye on what's likely to happen. It is not that the many are wrong in their analyses, but that they may be proven wrong because of their influence. They may so affect operations and plans of business (and of the public) that their forecasts fail to prove out. If you are convinced that inflation is going to accelerate you will manage your inventories and bank loans differently from what you would if you had been led to expect a slump. . . . So it is that economists may see their published predictions go wrong, whereas if they had kept them secret the forecasts might well have worked out with extraordinary accuracy.

Another reason why the theory of contrary opinion can be a useful tool for investors is its relationship to crowd psychology. When an idea has caught on among the vast majority of investors, it's likely that the idea is based more on emotion than on rational thought. Therefore, if we can learn to disregard or distrust the impulses and emotions that we feel (and are susceptible to as part of a crowd), then we have an excellent chance of being able to retain our logical thought process. But if we were to rely mainly on current economic and stock-market commentary, we would become victims of the crowd mentality. The best way to remain objective in the face of the powerful crowd pressure is to force yourself to think contrary to it.

Another, more subtle, reason why contrary opinion works is the fact that the crowd is rarely able to anticipate a change in trend until long after the turning point. Like Pavlov's dogs, when we become conditioned to a certain event, it's typical to expect the trend to continue forever. This is especially true when we are bombarded from all sides by propaganda that substantiates and solidifies in our minds the fact that the trend is in force. And it becomes very difficult to free ourselves from this Pavlovian conditioning, precisely because the fact is so easy to believe, and everyone else around us is in agreement.

But how does this relate to the stock market, and how can we see contrary opinion at work in the investment environment? Simply by noting how slowly investors become aware of a change in trend. As so frequently happens, the stock market goes up and up and up, and finally, after extensive gains, most investors are convinced that stocks will keep going up forever. But rather than look for maintenance of the status quo, they should focus their attention on when the trend will change. One of the certainties of life is that the world we live in, and the investment environment we operate in, are in constant motion and flux. Those who are always looking for the change in direction, and who use contrary opinion to do it, will be best suited to catch the trend.

Contrary opinion can also be used to determine how much potential buying power is left to come into the market. If all sides are bullish, and enthusiasm abounds about the prospects for stocks, the implication is that there is no one left to buy stocks and force prices higher. On the other hand, if skepticism abounds, there are still many market participants (presumably with large sums of cash) on the sidelines, who can be cajoled or tantalized back into the market.

Last, but not least, contrary opinion works sometimes because extremely one-sided opinion breeds unity. At the bottom in 1974, the Congress, the President, the unions, the consumers, the environmentalists, and the lawyers all had to join together to prevent a real catastrophe. In other words, if a fear is widely held, most everyone will drop what he or she is doing and unite. (This is effective even if it is unconscious.)

G.C. Selden, in *Psychology of the Stock Market* (Fraser, 1965), illustrates this pulling together in an analysis of the panic of 1907:

> In 1907, for example, the safest and best time to buy the sound dividend-paying stocks was on Monday following the bank statement which showed the greatest decrease in reserves. The market opened down several points under pressure of liquidation, and many standard issues never sold so low afterward. The simple explanation was that conditions had become so bad that they could not get any worse without utter ruin, which all parties must and did unite to prevent.

Contrary opinion need not be confined to the economic or stock-market scene. It works in other spheres as well. For example, contrary opinion and its insight into human nature was dramatically illustrated during the 1930s in England. Here was a nation so anxious to avoid war that it convinced itself, over the course of many crucial years, that compromise was the best way to avoid confrontation. But if, instead of compromising, Britain, France or any other Allied nation had taken an early and strong stand against German rearmament, there would have been no Second World War. Winston Churchill, in his book *The Rising Storm*, gave adequate testimony to that fact. There never was a war that was easier to prevent, according to Churchill.

In other words, had the people of any of the democracies believed, as early as, say, 1932–1933, that Hitler threatened world peace, they would have pressured their governments into standing up to him. Most historians readily agree that Hitler's military establishment could not have withstood an attack by the Allies up to and perhaps even later than 1936–1937. Of course, by the time Hitler's true colors became known, his military machine was so vastly superior to that of the Allies that no firm stand on their part could possibly have forced him into backing down from further aggressions.

Let's look at some examples of how contrary opinion can be useful in avoiding investment losses and accurately predicting the future. Almost everyone is aware of the inordinate overvaluation of the glamour-growth stocks in 1971–1972. In many cases, these companies were bid up to price/earnings ratios as high as 60.

Investors were betting that earning growth would and could continue at unusually high rates (such as 20 to 30 percent annually) for many years into the future. However, the risk of owning these companies was inordinately great, because investor expectations of these stocks were so high. No matter what the arguments in favor of these stocks at the time (and they were convincing), it didn't take a genius to detect the risks inherent in owning these stocks. And an investor who understood contrary opinion would have been very leery of making a commitment to stocks which were so widely popular and whose intrinsic value was so generally recognized.

Thus, whenever you hear only good things about the stock market in general, or individual stock groups in particular, be contrary and assume that a trend reversal could soon be forthcoming.

Real-estate investment trusts and bond funds, two of the more popular investments of the 1971–1972 period, are also a good example of the usefulness of contrary opinion. Although real-estate investment trusts as a concept had been around for a long time, they only became widely popularized when Nixon wanted to stimulate housing to get our economy moving again.

In that period, Wall Street sold real-estate investment trusts to the public in inordinate numbers. Certain banks, mortgage bankers, and others who had no business getting into the real-estate investment-trust business in the first place, raised money from the public to start their own trusts. Consequently, the managements of many of these trusts were sadly lacking in experience and knowledge of the real-estate field. And the money that the trusts raised was unwisely spent in bidding properties way above their basic value. This is typical whenever a concept becomes widely favored. Too many people enter the business, competition becomes severe, and a weeding out then becomes necessary.

Bond funds present a similar story. Here again, during the 1971–1972 period, several billions of dollars were raised from investors. But these bond funds proved to be poor investments in 1973–1974. To begin with, investors lost approximately 8½ percent of their capital investment right off, because the underwriters and brokers needed a commission to sell the deal. Beyond that, there was the problem of wide-scale acceptance of bonds as a good investment for the public (as evidenced by the popularity of the bond funds themselves). As we mentioned previously, such pervasive optimism should call an investments' credibility into question at once. In this instance, the bond market, and by inference bond funds, subsequently suffered one of the worst declines in a generation during the 1973–1974 period.

Another classic example of overpopulating an investment theme was the one-sided attraction to gold and gold shares in 1974. For many years prior to 1974, the people who sponsored gold were considered laughable because they insistently predicted depression and collapse. However, when inflation began to accelerate in the mid-1960s, and the British pound and the United States dollar subsequently suffered major devaluations, the concept of gold as a store of value began to capture the public imagination. Then, when the Arab oil embargo quadrupled the price of oil, gold bullion and gold shares took off to new highs. By February 1974, the price of gold bullion had reached $185 an ounce, and gold shares reached all-time highs.

Inflation, currency turmoil, and fears of a worldwide depression became increasingly prevalent as 1974 progressed. Everybody decided to get into the act. A whole series of publications on gold were born. Major Wall Street brokerage firms began recommending gold shares (for the first time ever, in many cases), and important publications carried numerous advertisements about gold.

It was clear that, at long last, the gold bugs were having their day. In other words, short of an actual end to the western financial system, the worst that could happen had already happened; the price of gold and gold shares had already discounted all the "good news."

But the propaganda continued. Americans were to be allowed to own gold for the first time in a generation come January 1975. Hardly a day went by without the media drumming home the potential effect of this new privilege. Gold was widely touted as going to $500 or $600 an ounce.

In fact, the consensus for gold was so great that a major network had a difficult time finding anyone who was willing to debate Jim Dines, the reigning king of the gold bugs, on the future outlook for gold. But in this very point lies the hint that gold and gold shares were no longer a good investment—at least temporarily. For, if no one can be found to argue the contrary view, then contrary opinion argues very strongly that the stocks for that particular group may be close to a peak.

Another area where contrary opinion proved effective was in the recent mania for "indexing." After ten years of underperforming the broad market averages, professional investment advisers decided not to try to beat the market anymore, but rather to "index" their portfolios in accordance with the weighting of the

152

averages. As a result, there was a reluctance on the part of institutions to own any stocks that were not represented in the averages. As luck would have it, beginning in early 1976, the averages behaved poorly, while the so-called secondary stocks (not in the averages) outperformed the averages by a wide margin. In other words, once again, the fad proved to be the undoing of those who participated in it.

Certain technical indicators can also be used in a contrary fashion. If one indicator suddenly becomes the sine qua non of Wall Street, it invariably loses its predictive value. For example, the Dow Theory gave what can be construed as a misleading signal in September 1976. Prior to that date, many analysts were saying that the bull market would resume if the Industrial Average closed above 1011, coupled with a new high in the Transportation Average. On September 21, the Industrials broke to a new high of 1014, confirming an earlier high in the Transportation Average. Yet immediately thereafter, the Industrial Average went into a tailspin and plummeted nonstop to the low 900s.

None of this is to discount the importance of the Dow Theory, or any other indicator in stock-market forecasting, but rather to emphasize that one cannot rely too heavily on any one indicator—especially when everyone else is watching the same statistic.

How does one become contrary? It is not easy, and it can be most confusing at times. Most investors on Wall Street recognize the value of contrary opinion, but very few know precisely how to put it into effect. One of the most popular technical tools is the number of investment advisory services that are bullish or bearish at a given time. If there are a preponderantly large number of bullish advisory services, then technical analysts frequently use this as an argument for the bearish case.

One can be misled by the simplistic use of such a tool. One can only take a contrary view of a subject if everyone else is truly bullish or truly bearish. If many technical analysts are referring to the advisory sentiment as a reason for being bearish, then those analysts themselves contradict the conclusion to a certain extent. For if they are bearish themselves, then the bullish consensus is not as widespread as they would have you believe. Investors must not only talk bearish, they must act that way.

It's possible to get quite confused at times, if you apply contrary opinion frequently. For instance, what would you think of the following: The market has recently had a huge run-up, and almost everyone is supposedly bullish. On the other hand, most of the bulls are aware that the market is due for a correction because of the large advance. Several well-known forecasters are quoted widely as stating that a large correction (of some 10 to 15 percent) in the market averages will soon be forthcoming. As soon as this view gets publicity, many analysts admit that a correction is possible. And, to add further confusion, several other highly respected analysts are taking a contrary view of the possibility of a correction. They claim there's too much consensus around for the bearish view, so the bullish one makes more sense. Confusing, right? Well, the market is this way a good 80 or 90 percent of the time. In other words, there is no clear and precise conclusion to be drawn.

It is well to remember that the widely held view is not always wrong, but it is invariably wrong on timing. In the above example, there was a widely held view that a correction was due. And no doubt it was due, but not when it was expected to happen. The correction didn't take place until six months later, at a time when most everyone had given up waiting for it. Thus, you shouldn't take a view contrary to everything you hear, only parts of it. Certain aspects of the widely held view may actually make sense.

Finally, don't expect the timing of contrary opinion to be exact. You may well find that you are months, sometimes years, ahead of the event. If you expect a long bull market because almost everyone is short-term oriented and lacks confidence about the future, it might take many months before confidence turns around enough to make investors happy about buying stocks.

Gustave Le Bon described it well when he wrote, in *The Crowd:* "It is needful, however, that these individualities should not be in too pronounced disagreement with received ideas. Were they so, to imitate them would be too difficult and their influence would be nil. For this very reason men who are too superior to their epoch are generally without influence upon it."

13

When All Else Fails,
Try Common Sense

"If knowledge is treasure, then wisdom is the treasurer. He that hath too much knowledge without judgment is made more for another man's use than his own." So the saying goes. In all things, judgment or common sense ranks high. In the stock market, it is as important as knowledge of human nature.

When you hear extreme talk (and, more important, when people begin to listen to it), it may be time to march to another drummer. Study the market and economy, and use your own common sense to see if the events that the majority think will happen can happen, and if there is adequate fundamental reasoning behind what they are predicting.

One way to use common sense is to observe how quickly the financial press takes up a certain point of view. (This in no way reflects on the financial writers themselves, but rather on the susceptibility of the ideas. Most publications by policy don't print far-out, iconoclastic views. Hence, only where there's some concrete evidence supporting a view is the story likely to be run.)

For example, in early December 1975, just three short weeks before the bull market took off in its second leg to carry the Dow Jones Industrial Average from 825 to 1000 in four weeks, the bearish thoughts of a well-known market forecaster reached the pages of a popular financial journal. This analyst, who had previously been bullish, suddenly changed his views. Within a day or two of that change, the financial journal had picked up the story and written about it.

This same thing happened again in March 1976. At that time, another well-known market technical analyst predicted a 100-point decline in the DJIA and advised investors to cut back on stock ownership. That prediction and advice quickly reached the pages of three or more major publications. As discussed earlier, the decline did not come as expected, not until almost six months later.

This is typical of the stock market; it always does what's necessary to confuse and confound as many people as possible. Thus, if it is obvious to the most uninitiated investor that the stock market must go higher, or must go lower, it invariably won't. The market will wait until such a time as a move in either direction is not expected. Sometimes, a little common sense can be useful in judging when these moments are apt to happen.

By watching the financial press and media, and listening to what others are saying, you can get an idea as to what is likely or unlikely to happen. In December 1975, for instance, it was clear that a decline in the market was unlikely because such a view was so apparently widespread that it even reached the financial pages of major newspapers.

Another very simple use of common sense is to note if it seems too easy to make money. No matter how brilliant or experienced one is, this is not an easy job—otherwise the market would always give more than it takes. Much study, analysis, and hard work are required. If all of a sudden one is making money easily and quickly, something is wrong. The market may be preparing you for a fall, trying to suck in larger and larger amounts of your money, prior to a collapse.

Imagine a young man with a poor investment record who

suddenly began to make money hand over fist in the market decline of the autumn of 1974. This man was short selling the high-multiple "growth" stocks, and then covering them at lower prices. It was all very easy, and in a few weeks he was able to make 50 percent on his money. Something was clearly wrong.

This easy-money period didn't last much longer—only long enough to sweep the young man off his feet and entice him into putting every dime he had into short sales. Just as his last commitment to the market was made, the market charged ahead. The Dow Jones Industrial Average ran up 100 points in two weeks, thereby causing the man to lose all he had made.

Many economists, market technicians, and investment advisors would like to make the whole investment and forecasting process very complicated. Perhaps it's part of the sales pitch: Things are so complicated here that you must have expert advice. Well, perhaps. But you need it not because things are complicated, but because your financial security is at stake.

In fact, wherever possible, one should simplify and use uncomplicated tools. If one cannot find tools that make sense and are easy to apply, then something is wrong. Why can't value be analyzed and ascertained with simple, basic tools?

This is where common sense enters the picture. If you believe that paying forty times earnings for a growth company is impractical, then you should not do it. Conversely, if you're aware that an annual return of 8% to 9% is the best you can reasonably expect from the stock market, why take a risk with stocks when bonds currently provide that kind of return? Or, on the other hand, if you find a particular company's products unusually appealing, then perhaps you should consider buying its stock. In other words, if you like the product, chances are others will also—which means the company should do well. In summary, listen to your own judgment. You may be surprised how successful the results can be.

Economists, brokers, and stock-market analysts are human too. They make the same mistakes as everyone else, because mass psychology in action applies to them too. It is important not to assume that people in the investment business are smarter or have more common sense than you do. In fact, the reverse can be true at times. Because they are all talking to the same people, and all concentrating on the same things, they are sometimes apt to miss the forest for the trees.

A classic case in point is what happened to the bond market in 1976. Bonds rallied very strongly through the first quarter of 1976, as the inflation rate came down. But then commodity prices started to move upward around March and, by April, the money supply was growing too quickly. The Federal Reserve felt it necessary to tighten up on monetary growth, which was exceeding its interim targets. Over the course of the next month, the bond market reacted very sharply. By that time, the media and many analysts around the country were focusing on every small blip in the federal funds rate.

The money-supply figures were placed under a microscope. (And all this in spite of the fact that the Federal Reserve states categorically that week-to-week changes in the money supply are practically meaningless.) Disasters do not take place under such scrutiny. The time to focus on something is when analysts and people in the trade are not watching something.

As it turned out, the bond market confounded all the bearish predictors by staging one of the sharpest rallies ever, from July through the end of the year. Here again, a little bit of common sense could have helped. It was obvious just by looking at the fixation on interest rates and money-supply growth that the country was moving into a more conservative posture. What's more, government, business, and consumers were very cautious about the rate of inflation and their financial security. They were certainly not going to go on any wild spending spree. For these

160

reasons, it was unlikely that there would be a resurgence of inflation at that time; hence, long-term bonds (still selling at record yields) were due for a rally.

Many investors make their fatal errors by assuming that an investment must be made now. The stock market is always there. In late 1974, most investors felt that the stock market might rally a little but would never recover, and that stocks would be flat for years to come. Yet, only six months later, the Dow Jones Industrial Average had risen by some 50 percent. Two years later the DJIA had almost doubled. And many individual stocks had tripled or quadrupled.

Therefore, if one were not certain about the future in the fall of 1974, one could have stayed out of the market until the horizon was a little clearer. If you do not understand what is going on, there's no need to do anything until such time as you do. (But don't wait until all the uncertainties disappear.)

If you're going to buy stocks, at least wait until there's been a shakeout of some sort. When you "buy on weakness" or after a pronounced decline, it is easier to hold onto your stocks through the next shakeout. You experience a nice feeling of confidence when your stock stays above the price you paid for it. (Of course, even though you buy a stock at a low price, it can go still lower.)

Good common sense or judgment requires patience, self-control, and discipline. These are three important qualities which investors should strive for. If one does not have these, one must develop them. Are we not all familiar with investors who do not have these traits? Do they not make a decision one day and then reverse it the next? Invariably, these investors buy when things look good, sell when things look bad, and, in doing so, buy at high prices and sell at lower ones. This is the type of action that investors must avoid above all else. It is frustrating and ruinous to their financial resources.

Many investors believe that the safest way to invest in the stock market is to have a widely diversified portfolio of stocks. There are certainly good arguments behind this view, but is such a strategy practical for the average investor? Isn't it better to own three or four stocks than to own twenty or thirty? The diversification argument runs into difficulty when it comes time to understand the fundamentals of all twenty or thirty stocks, especially if they are in different industries. It is nearly impossible for any one person to truly understand the diverse fortunes of twenty or thirty companies, let alone twenty or thirty industries.

It is easier to have one or two (and no more than three) investment themes. Look for the company that will benefit the most from the theme, and keep close track of the direction and promise of your investment theme. Constantly reevaluate the merits of it. Is the stock living up to the earlier promise it held for you? Is the growth or progress of the company measuring up to your expectations?

One last point: Don't be too rigid. Never fall in love with a stock or investment theme. One must almost be ruthless in one's objectivity.

14

Finding the Right Adviser

There is a fine line between acquired knowledge and the innate knack of making money in the stock market. Some people are born with a financial touch, just as some athletes are born with athletic prowess, certain writers have a born talent, and some scientific minds have the gift of creative insight.

As we've mentioned before, recognizing your limitations is a study in itself. It is the first and most important step along the road to stock-market success. As Flaubert said to de Maupassant, if you do not have originality, then you must acquire it. So it is with investments: If you do not have the qualities necessary for success, and are unable or unwilling to get them, then you must find someone who has them.

It was once said that the people who manage people can manage the people who can manage only things, and the people who can manage money manage all. But some people are clearly better at managing money than others—and if you want professional management, it's critical to find the one who's most qualified. In fact, selecting a first-rate adviser is one of the most important financial decisions you can make.

Typically, investors are led to brokers, mutual funds, or money managers by word of mouth or publicity. Because the record we hear about sounds so good, we often feel we don't need to dig beneath the surface to find out *how* the adviser racked up the good record, or if the record really is as good as we think. Just as we need to analyze the market, the crowd, and the underlying value of a stock, so we need to evaluate the qualities of a prospective adviser.*

Step one should be to analyze your long-range investment goals and to decide how much risk you want to live with. If you're close to retirement, then you obviously shouldn't be taking large risks with your retirement nest egg. On the other hand, if you're young and can afford some losses, then it may be worthwhile to be more aggressive with your investments. Either way, your first session with the adviser will be spent more profitably if you have a clear picture of what your goals are. You may discover, for example, that all you really need is an 8 percent return on capital per year. If that's the case, why take the risks of stocks, when you can currently get 8 percent or better with relatively riskless bonds?

Once you know what your investment goals are, you can begin your search for advisers. At each interview, the critical factor is to get by the sales pitch. (They are all going to try to put their best foot forward.) Too many investors get sold on an investment firm by the blue-eyed, blond-haired wonder who's a super salesperson. The thing to remember is that sales ability may have nothing to do with an individual's ability or a specific firm's talent at managing money.

To avoid falling under the sway of the sales pitch, you've got to take the subjectivity and chemistry out of the relationship. You may like the individuals and the firm a lot, but are they qualified to manage your money? The way around the chemistry problem is to ask tough questions. That way, the manager will have to stop selling and start thinking.

The first area to ask about is the firm's investment philosophy

*The following criteria are adapted from the author's earlier work, "Money Managers or Money Mongers," which appeared in the February 21, 1977 issue of *McGraw-Hill's Personal Finance Letter.*

and style. You'll want to know how the firm gets its ideas and what was responsible for its success to date. For example, the firm might have had three big winners in 1976, all of which were recommended by the energy analyst of a certain research firm. Suppose the success of that analyst recently enabled him to start his own money-management business—and now the firm you're talking to is high and dry.

Often, a firm may not be able to quantify the reasons for its success, which wouldn't be so surprising. After all, advice, information, and analysis come in from all sides, so how do you pick out the one source that provided the background for an investment decision? This is where philosophy comes in. If the manager has an investment philosophy (and there had better be one), you should be able to discover what it is. If it makes sense to you, and the manager seems unusually adept at putting it into practice, then you're on the right road.

Now you can ask how the manager developed that philosophy. Did it happen overnight, or was it worked up over hard years of trial and error (at other people's expense)? How long has the manager had this philosophy, and does it work in all kinds of investment environments. You'll want to make sure that the manager has firm convictions that don't change color with each new fad.

Once you understand the approach, you can ask how the adviser picks stocks. Is in-house research used exclusively, or are Wall Street and others also checked for information? Generally, the more independent the manager is, the better.

Be sure to confirm everything you hear with the junior people in the firm. (They're more apt to give you the true scoop because they're usually more open. In any event, check what one adviser says against another. You may be surprised at the contradictions that will crop up.) This is a good way to ascertain whether the firm actually practices what it preaches. For instance, the firm might supposedly be a big believer in market timing, but fail to sell stocks when it seems as though a correction is coming.

Next, learn about the internal structure of the firm. You'll want to ask about the firm's ability to adapt to change. Do the managers have the mechanism with which to cut their losses when they've made a mistake? Also ask about the firm's access to new ideas. You won't want a firm that's only receiving research on growth stocks when all the action is going on in the secondary issues. Be sure the firm also analyzes its investment mistakes and attempts to understand why they happened. That way you can be sure that the firm won't make the same mistake again. In other words, is the firm well managed? If there isn't good control in a tightly run ship, how can you expect them to manage money well?

Check out how often the assets in an average portfolio turn over, and ask yourself if what you hear fits in with your feelings about risks. The key here is that you want a manager who's an investor, not a trader. In theory, a manager who buys the right stock at the right price is not going to have to kick it out three to six months later. When that happens often, it implies a certain lack of conviction, plus a poor investment decision to begin with.

Don't forget to learn about the account structure. You don't want your account officer to be burdened with so many clients that your needs are neglected. (It's hard to imagine that an account officer could handle more than twenty-five or thirty accounts comfortably. However, many trust officers will have 200 to 300 accounts.)

Management's background is also very critical. The more diversified their careers, interests, and educations, the better. What's more, an international flavor is a big plus; many American managers tend to be too parochial, and don't focus on the international side of things. Since we live in an international economic environment, where nationalization of foreign assets

166

and currency devaluations are commonplace, that kind of narrow thinking could be costly.

Also look at the continuity and motivation of management. (By continuity, we mean how long the personnel have been there. A high turnover is a bad sign because it implies staff dissatisfaction.) It's important that the managers have incentives to do a good job and to come up with new ideas. Ideally, the managers should have a stake in the future of the business. That way, you know that they'll have as many sleepless nights as you do in a down market. In short, if you're giving your financial future to someone to handle, you want to make sure he or she feels a heavy responsibility to protect it and make it grow.

You should also check out the opportunity for "psychic rewards" at the firm. After a certain point, economic incentives may no longer motivate the individual. Or, just as bad, high tax rates may render additional compensation of little practical use. If a money manager is already earning, say, $80,000, what real difference would a $15,000 raise make?

What may be important at this stage of the manager's life is to be able to do the things that are more motivating than money. Perhaps these are writing a book, talking frequently to the press, doing outside consulting work, making speeches around the country, or being active in trade associations. Who knows? As long as managers don't get so involved elsewhere that they neglect their responsibilities, this is a good thing. A firm that allows such psychic motivation will attract and keep good people. You certainly don't want an environment in which people feel a lack of motivation and become stale. So long as they feel they are going somewhere, and pursuing what's important to themselves, they're bound to do a better job all around.

Integrity is also important. Ask for at least ten references, including the names of long-standing clients. Although you'll never get any bad references, you can tell a lot about the firm from the caliber of the references they give you. Also, does the firm have a sense of responsibility? Do they take their job seriously, and do they give the appearance that your money is just as important to them as it is to you?

Be sure that you really investigate the firm's performance backward and forward. Every manager can show you how XYZ account did better than ABC stock average. But don't let them sell you on their good accounts; ask to see the firm's performance over one complete market cycle. That means from bull market to bear market and back to bull market again.

One of the best ways to evaluate performance is to ask for a sample portfolio as of December 1972. Since that was only two weeks away from a major market top, you'd want to see a high cash position, zero growth stocks (which were devastated in the subsequent bear market), and a growing position in basic industries (the group that led the 1975–1976 market advance).

If the portfolio they show you looks good, ask for a sample portfolio as of December 31, 1974, which was a month after the bear market ended. You'd ideally want to see a portfolio with recent purchases of beaten-down blue chips or high-grade bonds with 9 percent coupons. But if the manager was fully invested at the top and completely in cash at the bottom, be skeptical.

Above all else, don't be swept away by the recent success of the manager. The market goes through phases which favor one investment style over another—and you're likely to get hooked just as the fad ends. For example, during the 1960s and early 1970s, a manager who was good at picking growth companies did better than the analyst who looked only at relative value. But now the tables have turned; assets, yield, and value are having their day. Hence, if you're going to be with a manager a long while, you want an investor for all seasons. In other words, does the manager's strategy work over a long period of time, and will it adapt to change?

By this time, you should have a pretty good picture of just how good the manager is. You should be pleased if you've received straight answers to all your questions. However, if the manager has been evasive and constantly avoided responding to questions that you asked four different ways, you should be really concerned about the organization.

If you're pretty happy with the answers you got, now's the time to get tough and put the manager through the wringer for one last time. Push out your chin, squint your eyes, and ask the following questions:

- What are your strengths?

- What are your five best investment decisions?

- What are your five worst ones?

- Who are your three toughest competitors?

And if the manager doesn't give you a satisfactory response to those questions, then go to the competitors and ask them the same questions. Sooner or later, you'll find the right adviser.

If you don't know where to start looking for a money manager, you can get hold of a book called the *Money Market Directory.** It's published every year, and it lists most of the money-management firms across the country, both alphabetically and by geographical location. In many cases, it also lists the amount of money the firm has under management. Start off by looking up some of the firms in your home town. If one appears particularly interesting, set up an interview and ask some of these tough questions. If the firm doesn't measure up, ask for the names of some competitors, and you're on your way. This may sound like an awful lot of work, but it is worth it when you think how much time and effort went into making your own money. Add up all the

*Published annually by Money Market Directories, Inc., 370 Lexington Avenue, Suite 2103, New York, N.Y. 10017.

years and hours of work you spent accumulating your capital, and then evaluate whether even 100 hours is too much time to spend.

If you have a large sum of money, it sometimes pays to spread your assets among several money managers. That way, you're diversifying your risks. Moreover, each manager will have an incentive to do a good job for you, because there's always the hope of landing the rest of your money.

But what do you do if you only have a small sum of money and yet still want expert advice? It's hard to say where the precise cutoff is, but investors with $50,000 or less (and in some cases, $100,000 or less) should consider the possibility of mutual funds. In spite of the dismal record of most funds in the past ten years, the funds are still a very viable alternative for many small investors. You can get professional management, for small sums of money, which would not otherwise be possible.

If you're interested in looking at a mutual fund, you should evaluate the fund's record very carefully. Look at its results over at least five to eight years. See how it did in both down and up markets, and study its current portfolio. Is it conservative or is it highly leveraged? How diversified is the portfolio, not only in numbers of stocks but in investment themes and industry groups.

Is the fund in the high-quality companies in each industry, or are they in the second- and third-tier companies? Get hold of past statements of the fund, and see what kind of annual turnover the fund had. Are most of the same managers still with the fund, or has employee turnover been high? (By the way, this is one of the great dangers of a mutual fund—that the one person responsible for a good record could pass away, go somewhere else, or start a new operation without your ever being the wiser. By the time you found out the truth, the new manager could have made some bad mistakes.)

Look also for age and experience. No matter how bright a young person is, it's often the old-timers who end up doing best on Wall Street. After all, if they're still around, they must have a strong survival instinct, considering the ups and downs of the Street over the years. Frankly, the older the person is, the better. The ones who've been around the longest are least apt to get caught up in some new fad (which could be very costly). They've seen almost everything there is to see, and they have a healthy skepticism.

Part Four

THE CHALLENGE OF THE FUTURE

Saving, capital accumulation, is the agency that has transformed step by step the awkward search for food on the part of savage cave dwellers into the modern ways of industry. The pacemakers of this evolution were the ideas that created the institutional framework within which capital accumulation was rendered safe by the principle of private ownership of the means of production. Every step forward on the way toward prosperity is the effect of saving. The most ingenious technological inventions would be practically useless if the capital goods required for their utilization had not been accumulated by saving.

The Anti-Capitalistic Mentality
LUDWIG VON MISES

173

15

The Importance of Capital
to the Stock Market

Everyone is aware of the fact that the stock market, as measured by the Dow Jones Industrial Average, has gone nowhere since 1966, when it touched 1000 for the first time. Hundreds of reasons are given: everything from inflation to currency problems to high long-term interest rates to a decline in real profits. All of these have influenced the stock market (as, no doubt, have a myriad of other reasons that investors would give), but they are not the causes, the real root of the problem. They are merely symptoms of the main problem which currently plagues us—an anticapital economic and political environment.

Before we can have a long-lasting bull market again, the attitude toward capital must change. There must be an incentive to save and an opportunity to invest those savings without a punitive tax structure.

A whole generation of Americans have now grown up without being aware of the significance of capital to their jobs, their standard of living, and their investments. This is a major problem, for capital is essential to all these things.

Let's use a simple example to illustrate this point. Imagine that you're a farmer living in the midwest during the late nineteenth century. You and your family have no modern tools or equipment because you don't have the capital necessary to afford them. All you have is an antiquated plow, some workhorses, and a few cows. You struggle along like this for years, unable to save enough of your crop to purchase another plow or more horses. Then, one year the weather is exceptional. You are able to harvest your entire crop; this is the first time ever that a part of it hasn't been damaged by weather or bad luck. You are able to take in more than you need, and you store the excess corn and hay in a special shed that you build for the occasion.

Winter comes. A prosperous neighbor, who was not so lucky as you in his harvest, asks if he can buy some corn. You work out an arrangement whereby you give him corn in exchange for the use of one of his plows during the spring planting season.

The next season, you have two plows at work and you're able to increase your planting area. Again, the harvest is good. This time you take in twice as much as you need, instead of 1½ times. You are now able to make a down payment on a tractor.

When the tractor comes, you become amazingly more efficient. You increase your planted acreage twofold, and the harvesting takes much less time. Pretty soon, you are able to afford a second tractor and to buy more land. Later, you buy a third tractor. Since you have only two children, you need to hire an extra hand. There are plenty of people in the vicinity who want to work for you. You pay a good wage, better than they can find elsewhere, because your tractors make your farm more efficient, more productive, and hence more profitable.

A business operates under the same principle. To have capital or savings, the business must make a profit—or, put in a nicer way, it must take in more than it pays out. If it doesn't, if it spends as much as it takes in (or more), the business will gradually deteriorate. This is what is happening to business in the United States. For years now, and to an increasing extent, our capital assets have been withering away. We have been spending more than we take in, and the stock market is a bleak but honest testimonial to that fact.

Many Americans think that profit is an ugly word. Perhaps it is, in the context in which people frequently use it. The implication is that one person profits from the other. This is not true. A highly profitable company, or a company that has a high savings rate, is a great boon to the economy. Those extra savings will be spent in part on new equipment and modernization which will increase efficiency and production, and thus lower costs, so that more people will have access to goods. The savings that are not spent will be available in one form or another as capital to finance the new projects or capital equipment of another business.

The mistake that many make is to think that profit means someone is being taken advantage of. Some feel that there is a fixed amount of capital in the world, and that it is transferred from one person to another (or from one country to another, or one business to another) through the profit motive. What one person has, the thinking goes, is taken away by another. For this reason, it is popular to think in terms of spreading the wealth, of preventing the gifted or ambitious from accumulating large sums of it.

But the profit motive does not work that way. There is no fixed amount of capital. The amount of capital depends exclusively on how much people save and how much they are allowed to save. And if tax rates are exorbitantly high, then people cannot save. What's more, there is little incentive to save because the capital they do put away is taxed at high rates. So it is that, at present in the United States, the maximum tax on investment (or savings) income is 70 percent, whereas the maximum tax on earned income is 50 percent. Who has an incentive to save in that kind of environment?

The first 150 years of our country were incredibly productive ones. As a nation, we worked very hard and accumulated much wealth and extra savings. The benefits of this hard work are currently being reaped, yet very few appreciate the importance of the efforts of earlier generations. As Ludwig von Mises says in *Human Action: A Treatise on Economics* (Regnery, 1966):

> We are the lucky heirs of our fathers and forefathers whose saving has accumulated the capital goods with the aid of which we are working today. We favorite children of the age of electricity still derive advantage from the original saving of the primitive fisherman who, in producing the first nets and canoes devoted a part of their working time to provision for a remoter future. If the sons of these legendary fishermen had worn out these intermediary products—nets and canoes—without replacing them by new ones, they would have consumed capital and the process of saving and capital accumulation would have had to start afresh. We are better off than earlier generations because we are equipped with the capital goods they have accumulated for us.

So if we continue to wither away our capital assets, as we are doing so hastily today, future generations of Americans will pay the piper for our selfishness. There is no easy way to modernize our plants and facilities and to replace obsolete equipment. There is no easy way to suddenly create jobs and make ourselves more efficient and productive. It can only be done if we are able to generate enough savings to pay for it. Says von Mises in *The Anti-Capitalistic Mentality*:

> The only source of the generation of additional capital goods is saving. If all the goods produced are consumed, no new capital comes into being. . . . Capital is not a free gift of God or of nature. It is the out-come of a provident restriction of consumption on the part of man. It is created and increased by saving and maintained by the abstention from dissaving.

178

Why then has there been such negative feeling toward capitalism (or savings) in this country, when it has clearly benefited so many, when our own standard of living is so dependent upon it? For one thing, the great depression had a lot to do with it. The previous excesses under unbridled freedom had been so great that society felt the need to protect itself from a repetition. So, over the years, a series of laws and government agencies were made to prevent excesses of freedom. (It is strange that many of these were instituted in the name of freedom.) Secondly, a change was in the air. A country never proceeds in a straight line; we'd had laissez faire and free enterprise, and it was time to try something different.

Last but not least, free enterprise is a harsh system, in a way, because there can be no excuse for failure to perform. If we don't succeed, that is our fault. Everybody has more or less equal potential for success. Under a truly capitalistic system, the man or woman of superior ability can go as far and as fast as his or her abilities will allow.

Hopefully, we are again being made aware (through economic necessity) of the need for savings on the part of business, consumers, *and* government. A shortage of capital can have far-reaching consequences—for the longer such a shortage continues, the harder it will be to accumulate capital and the more suffering will be required of those who have to do it. Says von Mises in *Human Action:*

> Capital shortage is dearth of time. It is the effect of the fact that one was late in beginning the march toward the aim concerned. . . . A loss in capital goods . . . makes it necessary either to abstain from striving after certain goals which one could aim at before or to restrict consumption. To have capital goods means, other things being equal, a temporal gain. As against those who lack capital goods,

179

the capitalist, under the given state of technological knowledge, is in a position to reach a definite goal sooner without restricting consumption and without increasing the input of labor and nature-given material factors of production. His head start is in time. A rival endowed with a smaller supply of capital goods can catch up only by restricting his consumption.

Hopefully, we shall see the error of our ways before too long. The stock market and our own children will pay the penalty, if we do not.

16

The Interweaving of an Investment Strategy with Income and Estate Tax Planning

In the nineteenth century, financial planning for business was a relatively simple matter. Emphasis was placed upon obtaining the capital necessary for expansion, and that was about it. Once the capital was raised, the money was spent and the business either thrived or went down the drain. But, with the coming of the large corporation in the twentieth century, increased international competition, and the growing need for capital and improved utilization of resources, financial planning for business became a more complex and intricate subject.

This same evolution is now taking place with respect to individuals and their financial planning. Twenty years ago—even as recently as five years ago—there were few comprehensive plans for, or organized approaches to, an individual's finances. One generally thought in terms of life insurance, perhaps a general estate plan, and some tax planning in reaction to specific and nonrecurring events. But this old way of looking at things is no longer appropriate today, just as the mere capital-raising function of business was not sufficient in the age of the large corporation. The many changes in our society and economy over the last ten years have created a totally new view of the finances of the individual.

If the old approach to investments (which focuses primarily on what to buy) is inadequate, then what is involved in the new approach? For one thing, personal financial planning must now add a new dimension of sophistication and overview. Previously, financial-planning advice came from a host of different sources. There were the lawyer giving legal advice, the accountant who talked about taxes, the estate planner who wrote the will, and the insurance agent who tried to sell life insurance. What is necessary today is a comprehensive look at the total finances of the individual; the right hand must know what the left hand is doing.

Furthermore, planning in a specific area, such as tax or estate planning, cannot be truly effective unless the area is analyzed in concert with an individual's total financial picture. How can you know whether growth stocks, municipal bonds, or a savings account is best for you without taking into consideration your income taxes and your estate plan?

Likewise, what's the sense in acquiring a huge estate, only to see it eaten up by taxes? The changes brought about by the 1976 Tax Reform Act will have a dramatic effect on certain estate-planning strategies. First, the good news: By 1981, by using all the benefits of the new tax law, you could pass up to $475,000 to your spouse at your death without taxes. What's more, an expanded marital deduction (the tax-free amount you can pass to your spouse) allows you to give your spouse up to $100,000 tax-free in your lifetime, and one half your estate or $250,000, whichever is greater, at your death. (Note that the $475,000 figure includes the marital-deduction benefits.)

The bad news is that the estate and gift tax rates have been combined. (Previously, the gift tax rate was much lower than the estate tax rate.) Even worse is the fact that whenever you make a gift, it ends up being included as part of your estate, for tax purposes. This means the advantage of lifetime giving is drastically reduced. The main advantage to giving now (apart from the $3000 annual gift-tax exclusion) is in getting the appreciation of any property you give away out of your estate. Thus, if you give away real estate worth $100,000, and it appreciates in value to $250,000 by the time you die, only the first $100,000 is included in your estate for tax purposes.

Worse yet are the new carryover rules for appreciated property. Formerly, not all the appreciation of your property would be taxed for capital-gains purposes, unless you sold it before your death. In other words, the basis for determining the value of property for capital-gains purposes was stepped up to the market value at the time of your death. So all the appreciation that took place between when you acquired the property and when you died was free of capital-gains taxes. No longer.

Your heirs now will assume the value of your stocks and bonds as of December 31, 1976, or your original cost, whichever is greater. The value of other forms of property will be determined by a special formula, on the basis of how long you held the property before December 31, 1976, and how long afterward. (Even worse is the new effective capital-gains tax rate. Under the new law, capital gains can be taxed at close to the top rates for earned income.)

Everybody's financial situation is unique. Thus, a generalization about all investors can be inappropriate as well as misleading. Furthermore, there are so many variables to be considered that easy decisions are rarely possible. But it is inevitable that more investors will begin to interrelate tax planning and estate planning with investment decisions. The earlier you get started on this the better off you'll be. If possible, find one person or one firm that is qualified to advise you in all these areas. They'll be able to run the numbers for you so that you can decide what course would be the best to follow.

Here are a few ideas to think about:

1. The younger you are, the more you should think about investing for the long term. (We'll discuss this in the next chapter.) True growth stocks are by far the best bet for most young people because growth companies provide a means for increasing your capital without annual income taxation. (Of course, when you do sell, any gains will be taxed at capital-gains rates.)

2. If you are in the later years of life, you do not have much incentive to assume the risks of growth. To begin with, the larger your estate is, the more it will be taxed. And any capital appreciation of assets will be inherited by your heirs, who will be taxed when they sell.

3. If you are a lot older than your spouse (and thus expect to die before him or her), you can and should use the marital deduction to shelter a lot of your estate from taxation (50 percent of your estate can go to your spouse tax-free).

4. It does not pay to risk capital for large gains, as it used to. Now that the capital-gains and earned-income tax rates are nearly the same, any gain on capital will be heavily taxed. And loss deductions will still be minimal ($3000 per year in 1978).

17

The Power of
Compound Interest

Even Albert Einstein stood in awe of it. One of the world's great miracles is the power of compound interest, said Einstein. If you're investing for a twenty-year period, the effect of interest compounding, or interest on interest, could account for nearly 60 percent of your total compound rate of return. In other words, if you spend all the interest or you fail to reinvest it, you are lowering your potential rate of return by some 60 percent. Yet few investors are aware of the significance of compound interest. And even fewer take compound interest into consideration when developing a specific investment strategy—which is a major oversight.

At 8 percent compounded semiannually, $1000 will double in nine years. It will grow to $7106 in 25 years, $50,504 in 50 years, and $2,550,749 in 100 years. And in 400 years, the original $1000 compounded at 8 percent semiannually would grow to over $42 quadrillion.

Of course, investors don't have a time horizon of 400 years, let alone 40 years. But if your time frame is greater than five years, you should incorporate compound interest into your investment thinking. And if your horizon is significantly longer than five years, say twenty-five or thirty years, you must consider interest as an integral part of your investment plan. This is especially true for IRAs and Keogh Plans, where the interest can accumulate tax-free.

The longer your time horizon is, or the younger you are, the more important compound interest should be to you. For a five-year period, interest on interest accounts for a relatively small part of the total pie: only 17 percent. But for ten years, interest on interest amounts to 33 percent of the total return. For thirty years, it accounts for 75 percent of the total, and for forty years 86 percent.

With this kind of progressive effect, present bond-investment strategy, which focuses almost exclusively on current return, can be turned topsy-turvy. For instance, over the intermediate term, say ten years, long-term interest-rate fluctuations will have little effect on the total compound rate of return.

Let's assume two extreme possibilities to demonstrate this point. The first, which is the "worst" case, is that long-term interest rates jump immediately to 13½ percent. The second, or "best" case, is that interest rates fall at once to 4½ percent. Then, for the sake of argument, let's assume that (1) long-term interest rates are currently at 7½ percent, and (2) we own a bond with a 7½ percent coupon maturing in seventeen years and selling at 100. Strange as it may seem, the best and worst cases have about the same compounded rate of return over a ten-year period.

If long-term interest rates suddenly rose to 13½ percent, the total compounded rate of return would be 7.6 percent at the end of ten years. But, surprisingly, if interest rates dropped to 4½ percent, the total compounded rate of return would be only a little higher, 8.1 percent. In other words, the capital loss on the bond that occurred when interest rates rose would be offset by the ability to reinvest at the higher interest rates. And the capital gain on the bond that resulted when interest rates dropped would nearly offset the inability to reinvest the interest at high rates.

Over a longer period, say twenty years, interest-rate changes matter a lot, in a way that you'd least likely expect: Lower interest rates present a much greater danger to the total return than rising interest rates.

If interest rates dropped immediately to 4½ percent, the 7½ percent bond used in the example above would only return 6.3 percent compounded over twenty years. But if interest rates rose to 13½ percent immediately, the bond's compounded rate of return would be 10.7 percent. (Neither of these alternatives, of course, includes the effects of inflation and the value of the dollar, but the end results are still more or less the same.)

Falling interest rates present another problem: Corporations could call in high-yielding bonds and replace them with lower-yielding issues. Hence, investors could get doubly hurt; their current return and their future reinvestment rates could be sharply reduced.

A good way to protect yourself against the danger of falling interest rates is to consider long-term United States Treasury issues. Although these issues cannot protect you against lower reinvestment rates, they can protect you against losing a high current return. That's because the bonds are noncallable for up to twenty-five years, depending on the particular issue. Hence, even if long-term interest rates do fall sharply, these issues won't be called in, as no doubt most, if not all, of the high-yielding corporate bonds would. (In fact, there are estimates that currently some $15 billion of long-term, high-yielding issues could be called in by corporations.)

Another good way to protect against the risk of declining interest rates is to buy deep-discount bonds. For one thing, deep-discount bonds are unlikely to be called because they already carry a low coupon and hence aren't costing corporations that much in interest charges. What's more, they represent perhaps the only way to partially hedge against lower reinvestment rates in the future. That's because deep discounts are less dependent on reinvestment of interest, since they already carry a low coupon interest rate. In fact, the better portion of their expected rate of return comes in the form of guaranteed capital gain.

But perhaps the best way of all to take advantage of compound interest is through "growth" stocks. The idea of growth or growth stocks is currently out of favor because the institutional favorites, the famed "nifty-fifty," have been such bad performers over the past four years. That's not surprising. They were bid up to unrealistic levels in the early 1970s, and we're merely seeing the reaction to that overvaluation. But that doesn't mean stocks of fast-growing companies bought at the right price aren't a good buy and won't do well in the future.

First of all, even if the United States is entering a period of "slow growth," during which we must learn to live within our means, certain companies are going to grow at the expense of others. Some companies are always going to carve out new markets, develop new technologies, and grab market share. Those companies can offer investors an excellent rate of return.

Second, fast-growing companies can show some amazing growth rates because of the effect of compounding. Since the compounding represents such a substantial portion of a total return over a long period of time, the greater the growth rate, the larger the initial investment will become. For instance, let's say you hold a growth stock over a forty-year period. At the end of that time, the reinvestment of the profits which that company generated could account for the substantial portion of the company's growth in shareholders' equity.

What's more, the return on shareholders' equity for growth stocks can compound free of taxes to the shareholder. (That's one advantage growth stocks have over taxable bonds.) If a fast-growing company reinvests all its after-tax earnings (which is likely if the company's potential is exceptional), your investment in the company is growing without your being penalized by annual income taxes. It's almost like a corporate pension plan, Keogh, or IRA, where no taxes are paid until retirement—in this case, until you sell the stock and realize the capital gains.

The opportunity to compound growth without taxes can boost your overall return substantially. The best way to illustrate this is by looking at a stock that remains flat in price for a twenty-five-year period but pays a dividend of 7½ percent.

If you didn't have to pay any taxes on these dividends and could reinvest the entire amount, 56 percent of your compounded rate of return would come from reinvestment of dividends. But if you paid taxes at a 48 percent rate, the portion of your return that came from dividend reinvestment would drop to 33 percent. Even worse, your total return would fall by 65 percent, even though you were paying taxes at only a 48 percent rate. Thus, the ultimate cost of taxation may greatly exceed the year-to-year tax bite.

For this reason, fast-growing companies offer the opportunity for a greater rate of return than either bonds or high-yielding stodgy stocks. But it's critical to find fast-growing companies with low investor expectations. Then, if the growth rate should slow for one reason or another, the stock isn't so likely to react adversely. This was the problem with the nifty-fifty institutional favorites. These stocks had been growing for so long and at such a high rate that investors could justify their very high prices.

But what happens to these so-called growth companies if the growth rate slows? Won't the investors who bought these stocks soon be dissatisfied? Well, that's precisely why the institutional growth favorites did so poorly. Their growth rate wasn't up to expectations. Now that "growth" is a bad word, perhaps it's a good time to look for fast-growing companies. At least, contrary opinion would suggest it.

18

Some Investment Guidelines

———

You understand the influence of crowds upon the market. You know how to keep your emotions in check. You understand value and how and where to look for it. But is this enough? In the heat of the moment or the glory of success, all the best intentions and most carefully thought-out plans may go awry. What we need at that time is a discipline which we will rigorously adhere to in thick and thin, some guidelines or a checklist to help plot our course across the difficult terrain.

In every discipline, there are benchmarks. The psychiatrist recognizes the schizophrenic because she has seen and studied hundreds of them. The professional writer recognizes an awkward sentence because his eye is trained to catch them. Dentists see cavities because they know what to look for. Students of the stock market also have some guidelines which they can follow. Here are some of the things to consider before you buy or sell stocks or make any decision in the market—a fail-safe mechanism, as it were, to protect you from yourself and the excitement of the crowd.

A FEW GENERAL POINTS TO REMEMBER

1. The changing situation within the economy and the perceptions, values, desires, and interests of consumers and inves-

tors ensure that no rule or system can ever be followed to the letter. There will always be a new set of circumstances to confuse and lead astray those who want to follow a simple formula set down in black and white.

2. A serious event may not be immediately recognized or perceived as such by market participants. Thus it was that the Arab oil embargo had little immediate effect on stock prices during the bear-market rally in the fall of 1973. In fact, the market even went up in the face of the bad news. But that doesn't mean that the market won't sooner or later realize the importance of the event and make up for lost time.

3. Don't necessarily sell a stock just because you have a profit in it or because a piece of good news relating to the stock comes out. The question to ask yourself is whether the next piece of news may be even better. It follows naturally from this that you shouldn't establish in advance a certain price at which you are going to sell your stocks. No matter what you do, don't pick an arbitrary price, for chances are the stock will go much, much higher than you thought possible.

4. Look for indications that all the sell orders are being absorbed easily, without any loss in price, or that all the buy orders are being met with sell orders, with no price rise. This could be an indication that some sort of change in direction is in the offing.

5. After a panic or a sharp decline in stock prices, don't expect the market to reverse gears quickly. It takes a long time to restore confidence to the point at which a rally can build up some steam. If you acknowledge that some time will elapse, you won't get worried if the market doesn't go anywhere immediately, and you won't buy stock options (if that's your interest) that mature in the very near future.

192

6. A common mistake made by market participants is to assume that one must be active all the time. The market is always there. If you miss out on one opportunity, another will come along again. There are usually two good buying opportunities per year. Thus, if you are confused, sit it out until you get your bearings again.

7. Watch for the investments or stocks that seem to appeal to the public's imagination. If one industry is suddenly doing very well, it can lure a lot of investors into the general market—which will benefit all stocks.

8. Don't be confused by trendless markets. And above all, don't let them trouble you or cause you to do things you wouldn't normally do. Trendless markets are those with about even numbers of buyers and sellers. The buyers are there in force and can absorb everything the sellers give them, but they aren't willing to rush in and bid the prices up. Hence, a trendless market. (It also works in reverse. The sellers can provide everything the buyers want, but they won't push the stocks out indiscriminately because they don't want to start a panic, where they might not be able to sell their stocks at all.) Watch the natural gravity of the market for an indication of which way the trendless market will go. If it keeps breaking through the top end of the range, that's an indication of the way it could ultimately go. And vice versa.

9. Making money in the stock market can be easy at times, especially at the extreme ends of a trend, when the rate of change is very great. But can you hold onto what you make? That's *the* big question. It can only be done through a careful assessment of the trend: Will it last? Is it suddenly too easy to make money?

10. Never sell during a panic. There will always be a rally when sanity returns momentarily, and you'll be able to get out at a better price. This was true even during 1929 (when there was a 50 percent retracement of the panic losses), and during the panic sale of gold shares in 1974. A 50 percent retracement of the loss is usually typical, but don't hold out for a full 50 percent move; settle for 40, or 45 percent.

11. Be most concerned with a market that is going down (or up) when you don't know what piece of news is causing the movement. In other words, if a market goes down and you know why, that's not so bad. But if everything is rosy and the market starts declining, be very concerned. The same is true of a rising market. Thus, the more unlikely the action of the market, the more you should pay attention to what it's saying.

12. Picking the right stocks is *the* critical factor in a bull market. In a bear market most stocks go down indiscriminately, but in a bull market some stocks do a lot better than others because their action is closely related to their profit performance or potential for profit. However, in a bull market almost everything goes up sooner or later, so don't be impatient enough to switch from stock to stock. You may find that you got out of a stock just before it moved.

13. The market spends a great deal of time backing and filling, either absorbing the selling or taking in the buying. At some point, all the sellers will be finished or all the buyers will have their quota; that's when the market will hurry to where it's going in a very short period of time. Try not to act during those frenzied periods, because your potential for profits will be greatly reduced. Do your buying or selling during the

trendless period, when you'll get better values. Buying or selling during a frenzy does not get you good prices.

14. Most stock movements go way beyond where they are expected to go. So it was that, during 1973–1974, even the bears expected nothing much worse than a decline in the Dow Jones Industrial Average to 680. But the Industrials fooled them and hit 570.

15. Fear is a much more potent force than enthusiasm. So it's not surprising that declining markets fall much faster than rising ones go up.

16. Most bull markets have certain unique characteristics. Certain stocks lead the way; certain indicators work while others continuously fail. Find out what the unique characteristics are, and watch for them.

17. Watch the importance of support levels and so-called significant price points. If a market cuts through these easily, it's worth noting. On the other hand, if a support level is broken and no selling follow-through develops, it could be bullish.

18. Be very aware of the danger of being too early on a trend. It was once well said that the graveyards of Wall Street are full of men who were right—too early.

19. The longer the corrective process is held back, the greater will be the resultant damage. This was the case in 1966–1974. If the government had allowed the economic advance to end by itself and find its own equilibrium, the ultimate debacle wouldn't have been nearly so severe. The same holds true on the up side. The longer the caution and pessimism are allowed to build up, the greater euphoria there will ultimately be when things look better.

20. Never be in a great hurry to get into the market at a bear-market bottom. There is usually a second "test" of the first low, and at least a four-month period when stock prices will back and fill. So be patient.

21. Ask yourself what is the least-anticipated event today. What would surprise the greatest number of investors? That event is what will probably happen, and you should always be ready for it.

22. Be prepared to see a really frightening market decline near the bottom and a phenomenally sharp rise near the top of a market advance. The market almost always looks best near the top and worst near the bottom.

23. There is a typical pattern to almost every market bottom, whether it is a bottom in a bear market or the end of a correction in a bull market. First, the market invariably goes lower than anyone originally thought it would. Then, most of the professionals become convinced the market has further to go on the down side. When that doesn't come to pass, the professionals claim that stock prices will continue to back and fill.

    For instance, the 1974 bear-market bottom went much lower than most investors thought it would. Once the Dow Jones Industrial Average broke 600, most professionals were sure the next stop was 525 (the 1962 low and the next support level). However, the break below 600 didn't produce the panic selling that the professionals expected, and the market rallied 100 points (from 584) in five days. Later, when the DJIA came back to "test" or confirm the bottom, it fell below 584, closing at 570. That created more pessimism. When renewed selling did not occur, the consensus was that the

DJIA would trade in a narrow range for a while. However, within a month, the stock market broke out on the up side.

The same pattern was true during the correction which took place after the stock-market rally that began in 1975. The Dow Jones Industrial Average rallied to 880 in July and came down to around 780 in late August. When the professionals realized that a correction was under way, many of them were predicting a decline in the DJIA to the low 700s. After the Dow Jones Industrial Average bounced off 780 on two occasions and failed to decline further, the thinking gradually shifted toward the view that the DJIA would trade between 780 and 880. Soon this trading theory became very prevalent, and within a few weeks the market broke out on the up side.

There are three conclusions to be drawn from all this: (1) Don't be too quick to buy stocks after a protracted decline. Stock prices usually go lower than even the bears expect. (2) Purchase your first line of stocks after the view supporting a further decline achieves widespread support and publicity in the financial journals. (3) Buy your next line of stocks when the consensus favors the view of a trading range.

24. If you must purchase the already recognized leaders of a bull market, wait until a barrage of bad news hits the group. And don't buy them until you've seen several different pieces of bad news and their effect on the stocks.

For instance, in the spring of 1976, the head of a major steel company predicted shortages of steel by the end of that year. This had thoroughly bullish connotations because a shortage indicated the strength of the demand and an ability to raise prices and hence increase profits. Thus, it would not have been unreasonable to expect the steel stocks to weaken—the good news was about as favorable as it could get. Subsequently, a multitude of ills befell the industry. Demand slackened, a price increase was rolled back, and profits plummeted. At each piece of bad news, steel stocks fell lower.

Conclusion: (1) Don't buy a previous leader in a bull market (which will have plenty of "profit-taking" ahead because so many investors will have profits) until investors are generally disillusioned with the group. (2) Wait until bad news no longer drives the stocks down. (3) Buy the stocks only when they go up on bad news (or up on good news).

25. One of the most helpful approaches to the stock market is to analyze investor expectations based on the most immediate experience. People tend to base their future actions on the recent past. Thus, if you know what effect the past had on investors, you can anticipate how they will act in the future. If the experience was deep and pervasive enough, chances are that the majority of investors will react to it in the same way. As we've said before, when the majority acts in a certain way, the odds are very high they are wrong. Here are some examples of investor expectations based on recent past experience.

■ Between 1966 and 1976, most investment advisers performed worse than the market averages. As a result, "indexing," or structuring your portfolio in line with the averages, came of age. If you can't beat the averages, join them, the thinking went.

Conclusion: The secondary stocks, which aren't in the averages, will show better market performance than the averages.

198

▪ Early 1975 and early 1976 were characterized by massive up-side moves. Great amounts of money in stocks (and especially in stock options) were made during these periods. As a result of this, most investors waited with baited breath for what they thought was another imminent breakout.

Conclusion: The "breakout" will be a long while in coming, and it will arrive only when everyone has given up on it.

▪ The 1973–1974 bear market was touched off by sharply rising interest rates and a soaring money supply. Because of this, investors will expect these monetary indicators to warn of the next bear market.

Conclusion: The next bear market may be caused by something other than tight credit conditions. For example, the bear market could be a result of a squeeze in corporate profits due to competition. Another possibility is that stock prices could decline dramatically before the monetary indicators give sufficient warning.

▪ The 1966–1975 period was characterized by boom and bust, an overheated economy followed by increasingly severe recessions. The bull-market advance following each recession was relatively short-lived. As a result, investors and economists are worried one moment about an economy that's about to overheat, and the next moment about recession. The longevity of the economic advance is frequently called into question.

Conclusion: This current economic recovery may last longer than most people originally thought it would.

SOME GENERAL QUESTIONS TO ASK YOURSELF

1. Are you overconfident because of a recent success? Have you thrown caution to the winds? Has your success in any way influenced your judgment?

2. What are your goals in a prospective stock purchase? Are they reasonable, or are you expecting too much? If the latter, then maybe you should rethink the proposed investment. There is no easy money on Wall Street, and large gains are unrealistic. Settle for realistic, achievable goals and you'll be starting off on the right foot.

3. Are you speculating about the future or are you buying a stock based on what is generally already known? If the latter, why are you buying the stock? If the news is already known, there could soon be more sellers than buyers.

4. Do you realize that you (along with all market participants) are prejudiced? Are you aware that you may only listen to good news and that you may play down any bad news relating to your investment? (And vice versa, if you're out of the market.)

5. Do you permit your attention to focus too much on your own investment? Is that diversion taking your attention away from where it should really be—concentrating on the action of the market and waiting for a change in direction?

6. Could you sell all your stocks today and, for the sake of argument, take the bearish view for a while? (And vice versa, if appropriate.) In other words, are you so inflexible in your view that you couldn't even consider changing it? If so, try altering your investment posture, and see if your perception of events changes in any way.

7. If you are thinking of buying a stock, be sure you know from whom you got the idea. What is his or her credibility? Was his or her conclusion hastily arrived at? Is there any hard evidence (of a psychological nature) as to why you should pay any attention to the idea?

8. Do you have a contingency plan in case your view is wrong? (The successes of a well-known investor were supposedly, in large part, attributable to the fact that he thought out, well in advance, all the possible contingencies that could ever occur. When the unexpected did happen, he was ready for it.) If you have, you won't ever get caught making a hasty decision, you will have a plan of attack, created long in advance, at a time when your rational mind was in full control. What's more, you won't be caught without a plan if your stocks suddenly sink. You will have an assured down-side limit because at some point your plan will go into effect and your stocks will be sold.

9. Do you have a store of excess cash available in case another buying opportunity comes up which is better than the one you took advantage of most recently? (For instance, your stock may go lower than it is now, or another stock you like may suddenly hit unheard-of levels. No one knows what will happen, so have a store of cash available all the time. What's the sense in always being fully invested?)

10. Do you trade by yourself, or are you following the crowd? Are you arriving at your own conclusions?

11. Do you loudly voice your own views? If you do, someone else may argue you out of your opinion, or your ego may get so hopelessly involved in your commitment that you can never get out, no matter how far things go against you.

12. Are you a generally optimistic person, bullish about the long term? If not, perhaps you should be. The economy and the stock market advance most of the time, and those who are optimistic will profit more in the long run than those who are always negative and cynical.

13. Do you think of your stock purchases as retailers think of their goods? (Would retailers buy something that they didn't think they could sell again at a higher price? Would retailers hold onto merchandise if no one else wanted it? No, they'd kick it out unemotionally. You must look at your stocks in the same way.)

14. Are you taking a gamble, or have you minimized the risks as much as possible? (True gamblers never take risks; they only get involved in "sure things." Can you say the same about your proposed stock purchase?)

15. If you think a correction is over and you want to buy stocks, do you watch the action of prices relative to volume? Do prices hold up well when volume contracts? If so, that's a bullish sign, and you can consider doing some buying.

16. Are you making the investment business too complicated? Do you rely on hundreds of different factors to make up your mind, or do you try to cut through all the details and simplify?

17. Are you making the mistake of thinking that the market doesn't already know any piece of news you hear? In 999 out of 1000 cases, if you know about it, so does the market.

18. At what time of year are you buying stocks? Is the natural seasonal movement of the market working for or against you? The market tends to move lower in the fall and late spring, and rise around year's end and in the summer. Are you

202

taking advantage of this, or are you falling into the trap of going against the seasons?

19. Are you expecting too much from the market? What kind of an advance has just taken place? Is it truly realistic to assume that higher prices are currently possible, without any intervening weakness?

20. Is it exactly one year since the last spirited advance started? If so, watch out for capital-gains profit taking.

21. What do the technical indicators say about the market? Don't buy a stock just because you feel like it; does the action of the market agree that this is a good time to buy?

22. Are you very happy with yourself, and are you going around gloating over how right you've been and how wrong everyone else has been? If so, watch out. That's a dangerous mentality, and you could be heading for a fall.

23. How many days of advances or declines have there just been in the stock you want to buy or sell, and for the market as a whole? Usually, some sort of reaction comes after five or six days of one-sided action. Don't buy after five days of advances or sell after five straight days of declines. Wait for a reaction.

24. Is everyone suddenly taken with your previously iconoclastic view? If so, then you'd better change it quickly.

25. If you're waiting for a correction in a bull market to run its course, look for publicity concerning the selling of stock by various money managers. The more they admit that stocks have been sold, the better. (The more investors who have cash reserves, the more money is available for the stock market.)

26. What technical indicator is everybody focusing on? Disregard it, and expect it to be very misleading.

27. How realistic are the prognostications for the market? If the Dow Jones Industrial Average is at 1000 and you hear people discussing 1200 or 1500, don't, whatever you do, buy any stocks. In fact, you might consider selling.

28. If you're waiting for a change in trend (a correction in a bull market or a rally in a bear market), wait until you hear the most stalwart holders of the view of the primary trend lose their faith. If they finally give up the ghost, you can be sure that the end is near.

29. Have you considered the potential effect of a presidential election? Is there likely to be a new president and thus hundreds of new policies? If so, be cautious. The market hates uncertainty, and stocks are likely to go nowhere, or down, until the new president is better known.

30. Watch very carefully when you see a decline in the market break a previous low point. Such action often signals a sharp rally, especially if no further selling of consequence comes after the new low.

31. What is the most recent and painful experience in the minds of investors and business people? Since that is what they will undoubtedly be obsessed with, you probably have little need to worry on that score. Look for problems or opportunities in neglected areas.

32. If analysts are lowering their earnings estimates of stocks, that's a good sign. If they're raising them, watch out. Contrary opinion applies to earnings estimates too.

33. What are investors paying attention to? In any normal period, there is both good and bad news (although one may predominate over the other), but the key is to observe what they're paying attention to.

34. What are the other major stock markets of the world doing? (We live in a world economy, and our market can't flourish if other economies and stock markets don't flourish.)

35. Be very, very alert when you hear that everyone is looking for a trendless market. It's just at such moments that the action becomes very spirited indeed.

GUIDELINES FOR INDIVIDUAL STOCK SELECTION

1. Do you think of your investment in a stock as if you were buying the entire company? In other words, are you buying assets that are reasonably valued? Are you also thinking in terms of a return on your investment? A buyer of a share of stock is purchasing a business and, therefore, should think in terms of the price of future earnings. If you think in these terms, it is very hard, if not impossible, to buy stock that is selling for thirty to forty times earnings.

2. Be very careful of fads in the market. This is one of the easiest ways to lose money. Therefore, ask yourself how publicized an investment theme is. How much recognition has it received, and how big a move has the stock had as a result of it?

3. What is the record of dividend increases for the company you want to buy? What does it yield, compared with the market in general, high-quality bonds, and other companies in the industry?

4. How did your company do during the last severe recession or shake-out in the industry? Did it perform better, in terms of earnings, than the competition? If it didn't, should you be buying it?

5. Have you studied or analyzed the top management of your company? It is management that makes the fortunes of a company, and you should try, if at all possible, to see the president in action. Go to the annual meeting or an analyst's meeting whenever possible.

6. Does the company whose shares you are interested in fill a long-term need? (But be sure this need isn't too generally perceived; otherwise, the stock may have discounted too much of the future.)

7. If you are thinking of buying a stock in a young industry, such as uranium producers, be sure to buy the companies that are already earning money. That is to say, buy the ones that are already demonstrating what they can do, rather than promising what they can do.

8. If you are thinking of buying a mineral or natural-resource company, think in terms of its proven and uncommitted reserves per share. That way, when you compare various companies in the industry, you'll be able to see which one has the greatest potential-earnings leverage.

9. Before you buy any stock, get a long-term chart of its price action. Observe carefully what its long-term pattern looks like. Is it now close to a major resistance point? If so, it may take many months or even a few years to break through. Does the stock carry a high enough yield to give you a sufficient return while you wait?

10. Don't be too quick to buy the stock of fallen angels. Those stocks may build a base for years, or go much lower than you ever thought possible. Wait! Time is on your side.

11. Ask yourself what is the current investing vogue. Is it growth stocks, yield and income, secondary stocks? How long and how pervasive is the vogue? If the vogue has been around for 1½ to 2 years and is widely publicized in the newspapers, chances are time is running out for it. That is the moment to look around for the next trend and to purchase stocks which will benefit from the change.

12. How does your stock react to news, both good and bad? If it sells off on good news, that is not a particularly good sign. But if it rises on bad news, the stock could be sold out.

13. Have you analyzed the stock from the standpoint of value? Be sure to make a comparison of value, as per Chapter 8.

14. When is the company whose stock you are thinking of buying going to release earnings? Has the stock gone up in anticipation of the earnings, or is it depressed because they'll be bad? In other words, could an earnings report offer you a better buying opportunity or a worse one?

15. What news is there which might affect the price of your stock in the near future? Is a union contract to be signed, a price rise slated, etc.?

16. Are you thinking of buying a hot group which has suddenly gotten a lot of publicity? If so, shouldn't you wait until the publicity stops and the stock reacts?

17. Have you checked to see whether the price/earnings ratio of the stock you want to buy is reasonable, and justified in terms of other stocks around?

18. If your stock breaks out of a trading range on the down side, watch it closely. If nothing happens, it may be a buy.

19. Are you buying a stock on good news or bad news? Is there apt to be more bad news or more good news? Never buy a stock on good news; always wait for a reaction before you buy the stock.

20. Does it really hurt when you buy a stock? Are you very, very uncertain that you're doing the right thing? If so, you're probably making the right decision.

21. Conversely, is it very easy to buy stocks? Does there appear to be no risk at all in stocks in general, and in your stock in particular? If so, you may be buying at the wrong time.

22. Have you watched your stock trade before you buy it? Do you know where support and resistance come in?

23. What has been the recent price action of the stock you want to buy? Has it had a big move? Is it possible you're getting in near the top?

GUIDELINES FOR DETECTING AN INTERMEDIATE CORRECTION IN A BULL MARKET

1. What is the level of investor sentiment? Are odd-lot short sales very low? Are specialist and member short sales close to 60 percent and 85 percent, respectively?

2. How pervasive is the feeling that the market will continue to rise?

3. Are the analysts quoted in the newspapers and magazines strongly bullish?

4. Are brokerage firms and advisory services placing ads in the newspapers which project a big rise in the Dow Jones Industrial Average?

5. Do most of the financial columnists discuss things from a positive point of view?

6. How far has the market advanced since the last period of market weakness? For instance, in late 1975 and early 1976, the Dow Jones Industrial Average suddenly rose from 780 to 1000—an area which had held back advances since 1966. It was probable that the market needed, at the very least, 1) a rest after such a strong move and 2) a large decline from which it could finally successfully achieve 1000.

7. Does anything look shaky on the so-called fundamental side of the equation? For example, the monetary indicators might suddenly have turned negative. Or, maybe the economy is growing at an unsustainable rate of 10 percent or more. (Such a development could not continue for long. The trend line is around 4 percent, and thus a long period of slow growth and flat profits might be in the offing. If this were the case, the market would anticipate the event and decline while the exceptional news was coming out.)

8. What is the *London Financial Times* index doing? Has it had a significant decline, or is it beginning to show some weakness after previous strength?

9. Are analysts widely raising their earnings estimates and putting many new stocks on the "buy" list?

10. Are analysts and brokers talking about unrealistically high earnings estimates for certain companies whose stocks have just had big moves? Is there so much confidence that analysts

are putting out earnings projections for two and three years down the road?

GUIDELINES FOR DETECTING THE END OF AN INTERMEDIATE CORRECTION IN A BULL MARKET

1. Are the sentiment indicators now bullish?

2. What happens to investor sentiment and the sentiment indicators on any rally? Do they quickly change from bullish to bearish? If so, the correction may not be over. For a rally to continue into something lasting, it must be met with skepticism and disbelief during a good portion of its move.

3. Do investors keep looking for a pullback in a market advance off a possible bottom? If so, it's a good sign. That means a lot of cash is ready to come into the market. But it is highly unlikely the market will accommodate these investors with lower prices.

4. Are some analysts predicting that the bull market is over? Have they received widespread publicity? Do these analysts quickly change their view if the market begins to go against them? (That's not a good sign.) Generally, the more strident and vocal the bears are, the higher the odds that a market bottom is close at hand.

5. The bottom of a correction is usually characterized by disgust, fear, or both. If you haven't felt either of these to a pronounced degree, chances are that stock prices will have to go lower still. The market will turn only when you're almost ready to throw in the towel. Are you at that point?

6. Has bad news come to the fore? As we've discussed previously, markets usually tend to make a turn amid pessimism and bad news. Thus, wait until the bad news begins to come out, and watch how the market reacts to it. Conversely, if the market or individual stocks go up sharply on good news, that is a favorable sign too.

7. Are the monetary indicators favorable? Are they suddenly showing unusual strength?

8. Has the *London Financial Times* index strengthened or risen to a new bull-market recovery high?

9. Has there been a successful "test" or approach to the recent low?

10. Does volume dry up on declines and pick up on advances?

11. Are there advertisements in financial newspapers advocating short sales?

12. Are the previously vocal bulls now very quiet?

13. Do the bears take large advertisements in financial newspapers advocating their position? In other words, are the bulls silenced, or at least modest and quiet, while the bears are self-confident and vocal?

14. Are the psychological characteristics of a bottom in place? (See point 23 on page 196.)

15. Have the excesses of the previous market advance been "corrected"? In other words, have the broad-based averages fallen at least 10 to 15 percent? Have the previous market leaders lost one-third to two-thirds of their entire advance? Have speculation and expectations of profits from stocks been cut back sharply?

GUIDELINES FOR PICKING A MAJOR TOP

1. Have interest rates moved up? Are the monetary indicators giving off very negative readings?

2. Is business activity booming, and is it as good as it possibly can be?

3. Have stock prices been rising for so long that investors have thrown caution to the winds?

4. Are all stocks participating in the advance? Or are only a few strong stocks misleading everyone into complacency, as was the case in 1929 and late 1972?

5. Are the newspapers full of optimistic news? Are the major concerns of the previous bear market totally forgotten by one and all?

6. Are you very confident in the future and totally optimistic about buying and owning stocks?

7. Is enthusiasm feeding on itself? Is this enthusiasm widespread and pervasive?

8. Is it now generally accepted that the stock market is a superior place for investment funds? Is this view now so widespread that it is no longer a subject for debate?

9. Are you so sure about the upward direction of the market that you feel confident about buying stocks on margin? Does everyone else feel the same way?

10. Is it the consensus that stocks have only begun their major advance?

11. What is the level of expectations? Have prosperity and overconfidence tended to influence judgment?

12. Have the country's cultural or social mores begun to reflect any of this overconfidence? Here are some of the social signs that were in operation near the last two major tops (1929 and 1966):

- A strong women's movement swept the country.

- The popular music and dances of the era were wild and carefree and emphasized an avoidance of responsibility.

- Women's hemlines rose to the highest level in a generation.

- Sexual restraints relaxed markedly.

- An intellectual arrogance took hold among the country's leaders. Certain immutable laws, such as "prosperity cannot continue forever," were forgotten or apparently repealed.

- Economic prosperity turned the nation's focus upon social ills.

- A "lost generation" of young people turned their backs on their elders' style and approach to life. This abnegation of background and upbringing was the most severe in a generation.

- The long road to prosperity was paved with government graft of one kind or another. Some form of major scandal came to the fore (Teapot Dome and Watergate).

- The birth rate fell sharply.

- Respect for institutions diminished.

- "Equality" became a favorite watchword.

- Expectations were raised to the point where people expected something for nothing, whether it was very

213

FIGURE 18-1

Major Market Tops and Bottoms

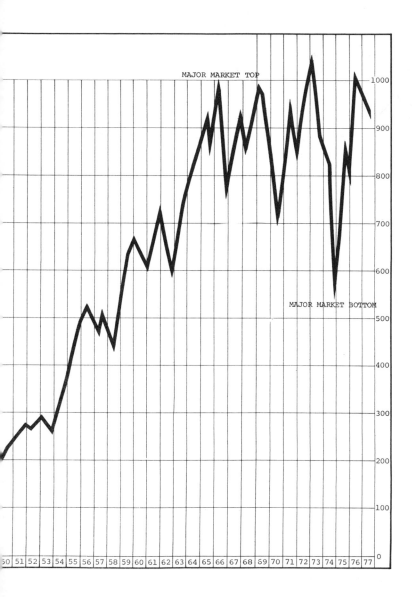

easy money, handouts, or a gambler's victory in the stock market.

- No voice loudly proclaimed the danger inherent in these raised expectations. And even if there was a voice or two, here or there, it was ignored or considered crackpot.

- Materialism and consumption reached the highest level in a generation. Consumers bought and bought, and competition for material possessions among families became quite severe.

- Religion and spiritualistic values declined. Materialism and the good life were more important than anything else.

- The country was hooked on unreality. Known truths were forgotten; the herd swept us all into some madness which we would never attempt in our saner moments.

- The trend that started at the beginning of the bull market reached a dangerous extreme, and no one appeared to be able to control it. In the late 1920s, the average American wanted to become a little capitalist and wear the shoes of the robber barons. In the late 1960s and early 1970s, consumption finally caught the popular imagination, and buying goods on credit was as common as buying stocks on margin in 1929.

13. Have stock prices begun to reflect this overconfidence? Here are some of the signs that will indicate they may have done so:

    - The yield on the Dow Jones Industrial Average will fall to 3 percent or less.

    - A dollar's worth of future earnings will be valued highly. In other words, price/earnings ratios will probably be

much higher than 14—the average multiple of the last
100 years.

• Closed-end stock funds, which usually sell at a discount
from net asset value, will sell at a premium.

• Brokerage firms will have back-office problems dealing
with all the stock volume.

• Thousands of inexperienced men and women will be
attracted by all the money being made on Wall Street.
In a short time, they'll be making five times as much
money as they are worth.

• A scholar will write a book or treatise demonstrating that
common stocks are a superior investment at all times.
(Edgar Lawrence Smith did so in 1924, and Professors
Lorie and Fisher in 1964.) A top is very near if the book
gains widespread publicity and attention.

• Every cat and dog in the market will have its day.
Almost every stock will sell well above its liquidation
value.

• The volume of stock trading on the American Stock
Exchange will reach 50 percent or more on the
N.Y.S.E. and remain there for a long time.

• A large number of public offerings for the account of
owners/shareholders will take place, indicating the tremendous interest on the part of the public in new issues.
(See Figure 18-3.)

• Public participation will be widespread. Everyone will be
aware of and discuss the fact that stocks have been the
best investment of the past so many years. (Today, for
instance, homes are discussed in the same fashion—
clearly a hint that the long-term appreciation in house
prices may be near an end.)

FIGURE 18-2

(Courtesy of Monetary Research Ltd.)

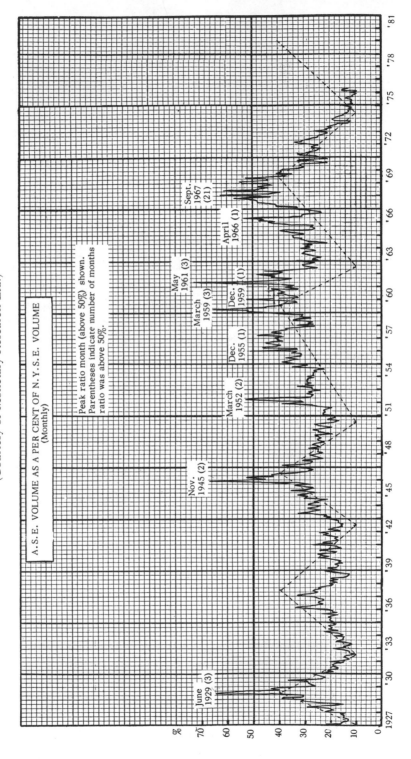

FIGURE 18-3

Secondary Stock Offerings versus the Dow Jones Industrial Average

(Courtesy of Monetary Research, Ltd.)

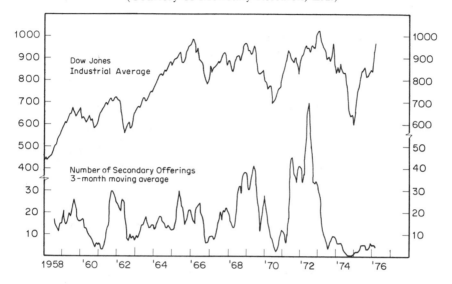

14. Are "growth" and "up, up, up" the latest words? Have consumers, businesspeople, and bankers been swept off their feet by overconfidence? Here are some signs that will indicate they may have been:

   • Buying on credit is widespread—not only in dollar terms, but individual terms. There's a feeling that lack of money is no problem; if you don't have the money, borrow it.

   • New projects, many of which are impractical to the objective eye are being spawned by bankers and businesspeople.

   • Money and credit are available for the most harebrained schemes.

219

- Many corporations are putting up fancy new office buildings, indicating their expansive horizons and self-confidence.

- Consumer demand is so heavy that large sums of money are being spent by business on capital improvements and expansion.

- The strength of the economy and the forces of speculation are so severe that the Federal Reserve attempts to spoil the party. More important, this action by the Fed does not cause widespread concern. The overconfidence is such that the majority of investors and businesspeople retain their optimism in the face of a clear tightening move, which in periods of caution would be considered a serious cause for alarm.

- Long- and short-term interest rates move up considerably. Neither event causes much concern among investors and businesspeople, who are mesmerized by prosperity.

15. Have the indicators turned negative? What has happened to the specialist short-sales ratio, member short-sales ratio, odd-lot short-sales ratio? To monetary indicators? To the *London Financial Times* index? The Dow Theory? Confirmation indicators? Has the market breadth weakened? Is the average stock faring much worse than the Dow Jones Industrial Average? Has the market had a sharp upward spike (or "blowoff")—a typical occurrence at tops?

GUIDELINES FOR PICKING A MAJOR BOTTOM

1. Have monetary conditions started to ease? Are the Dow Jones Utility Average, Dow Jones 20-Bond Averages, and the

government bond market all advancing nicely after the previous declines?

2. Is the economic news starting to get bad? Are major publications devoting cover stories to the forthcoming decline in economic activity?

3. Are all stocks declining together, especially the high flyers of the previous bull market? The sharper and more pervasive the declines, the closer the bottom is.

4. Are professionals who had been waiting to buy stocks now convinced that the market will go lower still? Is that conviction now so widely assumed that it's no longer even a subject for debate?

5. What's happening to volume? Has it slowed dramatically from the previous peak? (For instance, the 1974 and 1932 bottoms occurred on greatly reduced volume.)

6. Are you so turned off by stocks that you want to hide your money under a mattress?

7. What are the other world stock markets doing? Have they stopped declining? Are any of them rising yet?

8. How do stocks react to bad news? If they hold their ground in the face of sharply declining business earnings or a dividend cut, it's a good sign.

9. Can you find anyone who is advocating the purchase of stocks? If so, is anybody listening?

10. Has the market made a "test" of its bottom? Has it come back to the low and proved that it wants to bottom? Do investors get even more scared at this test? If so, that's a good sign.

11. Have the so-called glamour stocks of the previous bull market taken a real beating? (These are usually the last to decline because defensive money will seek a haven in the quality companies.) You want to see all these stocks decline together. Normally, they should lose at least 50 percent of the value they had at the top of the market.

12. Have the broad-based, unweighted averages (when deflated by consumer prices in inflationary times) fallen by 65 to 75 percent or more?

13. Have stock prices declined enough to correct the previous period's excesses? Or has the duration of the decline achieved the same result?

14. Have most of your acquaintances who own stocks liquidated some or all of what they hold?

15. Is the brokerage business consolidating and going through a major contraction and elimination of the previous period's excesses?

16. Do stocks show a resistance to further decline? In other words, does the number of unchanged issues on the New York Stock Exchange reach 500 or more daily?

17. Has the decline of up-side/down-side volume on the New York Stock Exchange reversed itself? (See Figure 18-4.)

18. Has market breadth turned positive?

19. Have the sentiment indicators turned positive?

20. Is it very easy to make money by short selling stocks? Can you indiscriminately pick a high-multiple stock, short it, and quickly make money?

21. Has a major low which held for at least two to four years been broken? When that happened, did the majority of investors look for further significant price declines? (Note that the October 1974 bottom came shortly after the 1970 bottom was broken. The final bottom in December 1974 occurred immediately after the October low was breeched. It seems that breaking a previous low is psychologically very important. (See Figure 18-5.) Thus, it always pays to think in terms of the prior low in the Averages, and to watch what happens when that is broken.

22. Have worries concerning the economy increased considerably? Has debate about the economy shifted from whether there might be a recession to whether there will be a depression? (It is worthwhile to note that stock prices generally fall by 50 percent of what will be their total decline before much bad economic news comes to the fore. Thus, as mentioned previously, a good measure of how much further stock prices must decline is the amount of bad news that has come out.)

23. Has the yield on the Dow Jones Industrial Average risen to at least 6 percent? No bear market in this century has ended before dividend yields on the Dow Jones Industrial Average reached 6 percent. (Of course, there's no reason why yields couldn't go considerably higher.)

24. Has the market had at least three downward steps? (As discussed earlier, some analysts believe the market moves in steps of three. This proved to be the case in the 1973–1974 bear market; there were three downward steps. More important, there were three major declines after the bull market ended in 1966. There were the 1966 drop, the 1969–1970 decline, and the washout in 1973–1974.

FIGURE 18-4
Up-side/Down-side Volume
(Courtesy of Monetary Research Ltd.)

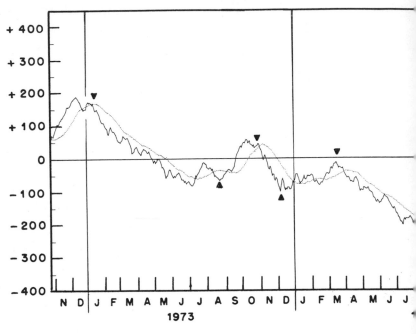

▼ Peak in DJIA

▲ Trough in DJIA

25. Has the *London Financial Times* index begun to strengthen?

26. Have interest rates begun to decline, thereby confirming the beginning of a slackening in business activity?

You've been through the checklist, and hopefully you have a fail-safe mechanism which will help you to avoid major errors. But all the knowledge and experience in the world can amount to

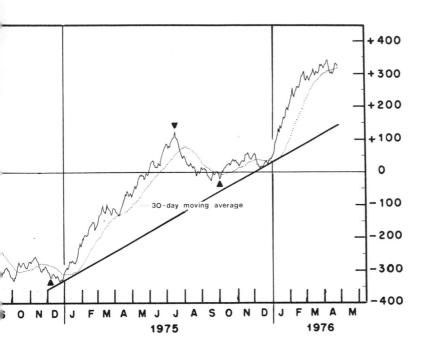

nothing when we have been too successful. At such times, over-confidence can ruin us. As Henry Howard Harper says in *The Psychology of Speculation* (Fraser Publishing, 1966):

> An enormous amount of stock market speculators become victims of over-confidence after a series of successful trades. Their buoyant spirits increase with every new success, until at length they throw discretion to the winds, extend their risks far beyond the margin of safety, and at the infallible turn of the market they find themselves in

225

FIGURE 18-5

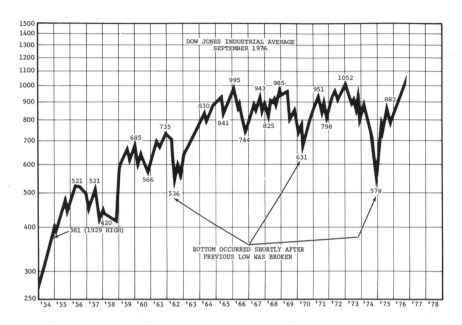

difficulty, like foolish fishes that get stranded on the beach at high tide. . . . Prosperity in the stock market seems to encourage optimism, rashness and impatience in about the same degree that adversity discourages enterprise and aspiration. But there is far greater danger in excessive optimism than in excessive pessimism, for the reason that optimists are inclined to back their hopeful views by indiscriminate purchases of stocks at high prices, while pessimists are seldom disposed to back their views at all.

Thus, in the stock market, like nowhere else in life, nothing succeeds worse than success. If you can remember *that* at all times, the odds against you in the stock market can be sharply reduced.

Selected References

Will Durant, *The Mansions of Philosophy*, Simon & Schuster, New York, 1929.

Edson Gould, *Findings and Forecasts*, published bimonthly, by Anametrics, Inc., 30 Rockefeller Plaza, New York, 10020.

Henry Howard Harper, *The Psychology of Speculation*, Fraser Publishing Co., Wells, Vermont, 1966.

Fred C. Kelly and Sullivan Burgess, *How Shrewd Speculators Win*, Fraser Publishing Co., Wells, Vermont, 1969.

Gustave Le Bon, *The Crowd*, Macmillan, New York, 1960.

Charles Mackay, *Extraordinary Popular Delusions and the Madness of Crowds*, Farrar, Straus & Giroux, New York, 1932.

Humphrey B. Neill, *The Art of Contrary Thinking*, 4/e, The Caxton Printers, Ltd., Caldwell, Idaho, 1971.

Richard Russell, *Dow Theory Letters*, published biweekly, P.O. Box 1759, LaJolla, California 92038.

G. C. Selden, *Psychology of the Stock Market*, Fraser Publishing Co., Wells, Vermont, 1965.

Boris Sokoloff, *Napoleon: A Doctor's Biography*, Prentice-Hall, Inc., New York, 1937.

Robert L. Smitley, *Popular Financial Delusions*, Fraser Publishing Co., Wells, Vermont, 1963.

Ludwig von Mises, *The Anti-Capitalistic Mentality*, Libertarian Press, South Holland, Illinois, 1972.

———, *Human Action: A Treatise on Eonomics*, 3/e, Henry Regnery Co., Chicago, Illinois, 1966.

INDEX

Index